无界BORDERLESS
社区COMMUNITY

米笑（Michelle Yip）　［澳］何志森（Jason Zhisen Ho）　著

华南理工大学出版社
SOUTH CHINA UNIVERSITY OF TECHNOLOGY PRESS
·广州·

图书在版编目（CIP）数据

无界社区：汉英对照 / 米笑，（澳）何志森（Jason Zhisen Ho）著 . — 广州：华南理工大学出版社，2022.12
ISBN 978-7-5623-6795-6

Ⅰ.①无⋯　Ⅱ.①米⋯②何⋯　Ⅲ.①文化产业 – 研究 – 番禺区 – 汉、英　Ⅳ.①G124

中国版本图书馆 CIP 数据核字（2022）第 098772 号

无界社区

米　笑　（澳）何志森　著

出 版 人：柯　宁
出版发行：华南理工大学出版社
　　　　　（广州五山华南理工大学 17 号楼，邮编 510640）
　　　　　http://hg.cb.scut.edu.cn　E-mail: scutc13@scut.edu.cn
　　　　　营销部电话：020-87113487　87111048（传真）
责任编辑：周　芹
翻　　译：程　倩
装帧设计：江俊颖、曾莹、何志森、臧立平 @typo_d
责任校对：梁樱雯
印 刷 者：广州市新怡印务股份有限公司
开　　本：787mm × 1092 mm　1/16　印张：15.5　插页：2　字数：510 千
版　　次：2022 年 12 月第 1 版　2022 年 12 月第 1 次印刷
定　　价：268.00 元

版权所有　盗版必究　　印装差错　负责调换

序一

何镜堂 He Jingtang

中国工程院院士
全国勘察设计大师
梁思成建筑奖获得者
华南理工大学建筑设计研究院有限公司
董事长、首席总建筑师

Academician of Chinese Academy of Engineering
National Survey and Design Master
Liang Sicheng Architecture Prize Laureate
Chairman and Chief Architect of SCUT Architectural Design and Research Institute Co., Limited

叶敏①是我女儿的中学同学。可能受我的影响,华南师范大学附属中学当年有7个学生考上华南理工大学建筑学系,叶敏是其中一个。后来叶敏考上了我和许安之老师的研究生。当时住宅建设开始走向市场化,国家很需要这方面的人才,我就建议她以"小康型高层住宅设计探讨"为硕士论文题目。

大概 2006 年,她成立自己的事务所扉建筑后,便常邀请我去看她的作品,像亿达大厦、星海音乐厅系列改造、二沙岛文立方、四海寒舍等项目,都小而精,有创新,有理念。尤为独特的是她还创办了一家公益艺术机构——扉美术馆,通过举办一系列公众参与的社会艺术讲座、展览来不断丰富建筑和建筑学学科,设计建筑,更顾及人。其中的"菜市场美术馆"项目获邀参展 2021 年的威尼斯建筑双年展,并在《三联生活周刊》发起的首届人文城市奖活动中被选为社区营造首推案例。主持该项目的馆长何志森博士也是华工建筑学院的年轻研究员。叶敏和她的同事们通过这些项目为建筑师们提供了很好的重新思考建筑意义的机会。她的"艺术营造"无界建筑理念不仅继承了我提出的整体观和可持续发展观,也以独特的方式赋予了建筑文化性。扉建筑逐渐成为一家具有独特理念和鲜明风格的建筑事务所。

她带领团队设计的"紫泥十二门无界社区"业界反响非常好,完全打破了一般房地产项目"千楼一面"的桎梏。其内部空间的处理特别丰富,创造了很多立体的邻里空间;外立面的设计让人印象尤为深刻;在标准化的柱网内根据住户

---

① 米笑(Michelle Yip)为叶敏的笔名。

提出的使用需求搭建了各种灵活可变的建筑构件，形成材料和空间异常丰富的立面，展现了当前年青人别具一格的生活方式；各个立面的处理也都有考虑到节能环保的因素，整体非常符合南方地区气候特点，具有鲜明的时代性和地域性，反映了当前人们对住宅的需求已经从小康社会的工业化迈向富裕社会的个性化。这一项目能与国际顶尖事务所同台竞争并赢得两个建筑界重要的国际大奖，说明无界社区指示了一种未来居住的趋势，对未来房地产开发有很好的示范作用。

作为叶敏的导师，我很赞赏她在毕业后能沿着自己喜欢和认同的方向坚持创作，有理念、有实践、有抱负，不断追求创新，不断突破边界，实在难能可贵，是同辈青年建筑师中的佼佼者。

祝贺叶敏，以及扉的小伙伴们。

何镜堂

2022 年 7 月

Preface I

Michelle Yip was my daughter's high school (The Affiliated High School of South China Normal University) classmate. Perhaps, owing to my inadvertent influence, there were seven students in their grade (including Michelle) ended up studying architecture in South China University of Technology (SCUT). Eventually, Michelle became me and Xu Anzhi's graduate student. It was the time when residential property market began to appear in China and talent in the field was in great need. I suggested Michelle theme her master degree thesis on "Highrise Residential Buildings for Middle-income People".

Michelle established her design studio, FEI Architects, in 2006. Since then, she often invited me to see her works such as Estate Plaza (an office building), renovations of Xinghai Concert Hall, Ersha Island Man Lap Fong (a shopping mall) and Si Hai Han She (a restaurant complex). Without exception, they are elegant innovative modestly-sized projects with distinct design concepts. Most unusually, Michelle founded a non-profit art institute, FEI Arts Museum. Through continual series of participatory public art events such as seminars and exhibitions, she enriches both buildings and architecture with humanity. Among the projects, the Market Museum project participated in the Venice Architecture Biennale 2021 and was shortlisted as a Community Empowerment Exemplar of the first City for Humanity Awards initiated by *Sanlian Lifeweek Magazine*. Dr. Jason Zhisen Ho, the curator of the project, is also a young researcher at the School of Architecture of SCUT. Michelle and her colleagues provide a good opportunity for architects to rethink the meaning of architecture through these projects. Her borderless concept of "Artecture", which combines art and architecture, not only inherits my holistic view and sustainable development idea on architecture, but also gives it a unique cultural dimension. FEI Architects becomes an architectural firm with unique conception and distinctive style.

The Borderless Community of Zi Ni Twelve Portals designed by Michelle and her team, which completely breaks the "one-facade-fits-all" approach of usual real estate projects, elicited very positive response from the industry. The treatment of internal space is complex and varied, creating a lot of three-dimensional neighborhood space. The design of the facade is particularly impressive. Within a common grid of columns, various versatile space modules are designed according to the needs of residents, creating elevations that are exceptionally prolific and diversified in material and space usage and suits the unique lifestyle of young people today. The design of elevations and modules takes into account energy-saving and environmental factors, which in general is very well-suited to the climate of southern China and reflects distinctively the characteristics of the times and regionality. It also reflects the evolution of people's housing demand from standardized design of modestly well-off society to personalized design of affluent society. The fact that the Borderless Community project competed well with projects of some world-class architects and won two important international awards shows that it indicates a future trend of living and is a pioneering example for future real estate development.

As Michelle's mentor, I appreciate her persistence in working hard in fields she believes and loves. She has her own ideas and keeps practicing them. With amazing aspiration, she pursues innovation and keeps breaking boundaries. These are valuable qualities that make her an outstanding young architect of her generation.

Congratulations to Michelle and her young fellows of FEI!

July, 2022

序二

许安之 Xu Anzhi

首届"深圳市工程勘察设计功勋大师"
深圳大学建筑与土木工程学院首任院长、前设计院院长兼总建筑师
国家一级注册建筑师
麦吉尔大学访问学者

Meritorious Master of the First Shenzhen Engineering Survey and Design Award
Founding Dean of the School of Architecture and Civil Engineering, previous Dean and Chief Architect of the Design Institute of Shenzhen University
National First-class Registered Architect
Visiting Scholar of McGill University

叶敏在读研究生时有两位导师,这是很少见的。20世纪90年代初,我所在的深圳大学建校还不到十年,国家教委指示我校的建筑学专业可与华南理工大学联合培养研究生,这才有了叶敏的奇特学业经历。她是我和华南理工大学联合指导的第二位研究生,研究方向是住宅。

住宅是人类自古以来最基本的建筑类型。为本书写序,正逢全世界出门几乎都要戴口罩并尽量与人保持一定距离的独特年代,也就是说,我是在特别"有界"的环境下来写"无界"之序,别有一番感受。

现代社会发展使人们生活多样化、职业多样化、个性多样化,这是社会发展和进步的表现。

自1960年代荷兰建筑师约翰·哈勃肯(John Habraken)提出"开放式建筑"宣言,现代住宅运动的创新针对社会住宅缺乏个性和多样性,强调居住者参与设计的"开放式住宅"的理念,一直是建筑师尝试和关注的方向。

叶敏的作品清晰地表达了这种理念,她以独特的视角抓住了广东番禺一大型糖厂在社会变迁转型期的机遇,在城市更新的大背景下,做了这次有益的尝试。她的"紫泥十二门"项目呈现了一种归属岭南沃土成长出来的丰饶气息,看似平常的语汇被巧妙地糅合进不寻常的建筑体中。如果没有她持续对社区文化和设计等的热爱和投入,这个项目是无法呈现这种独特魅力的。

除了紫泥十二门，叶敏创办的扉美术馆也在用"建筑之外"的方法实现另类"无界社区"。馆长何志森博士是位面向社区的模范建筑师。他把西方建筑学教育体系当中的社会学、人类学等研究方法应用在公共空间的营造上，以"不造物"的方式拓展空间的公共性。特别值得一提的是"菜市场美术馆"带给建筑师对公共建筑的多维思考。

期待未来有更合理灵活的法规能使她现在的小规模的共居形态，转化为更多使用者能真正体验自定义的领域空间，使批量化又多样化的"无界社区"的理念得以实现。同时期望建筑师能从"菜市场美术馆"项目获得启发，在城市更新方面产生更多元的建筑方法。

2022 年 7 月

Preface II

It's quite unusual for Michelle Yip to have two supervisors as a postgraduate student. In the early 1990s, Shenzhen University, where I worked and which had been founded for less than ten years, was directed by the State Education Commission to provide its postgraduate education in architecture jointly with South China University of Technology, and hence Michelle had her unique academic experience. She was my second postgraduate student under this "double-supervisors system" and her research direction was in housing.

Housing has been the most basic type of architecture since time immemorial in human history. I'm writing the preface to this book, in a unique time when almost everyone in the world has to wear mask and observe the social distance rule while going out. I'm actually writing something about "borderless" in a particularly "bounded" environment, which gives me a peculiar feeling.

The development of modern society has made people's life, occupation and personality more diversified, which is the manifestation of social development and progress.

In 1960s, John Habraken, a Dutch architect, initiated the "Open Building" idea. In view of the lack of individuality and diversity in building design, the Innovation of Modern Housing Movement emphasized the concept of "Open Housing" featuring participation of residents in architectural design. It has always been the direction that architects follow.

Michelle's work clearly captures this idea. With a unique perspective, she uses the project in a large sugar factory in Panyu, Guangdong, which had gone through drastic social change and transformation, to make a beneficial attempt under the backdrop of urban renewal. Her Zi Ni Twelve Portals project demonstrates a distinctive style deeply rooted in the Lingnan culture, where seemingly ordinary architectural expressions are skillfully blended into an extraordinary architecture. Without her ardent passion for and persistent devotion to community culture and design, it is impossible for the project to exude such a unique charm.

In addition to Zi Ni Twelve Portals, FEI Arts Museum, founded by Michelle, also adopts a method of "beyond architecture" to create an alternative "borderless community". The curator, Dr. Jason Zhisen Ho, is a model architect in the area of community empowerment. He applies the research methods of sociology and anthropology in the western architectural education system to the construction of public space, and expands the publicness of space in a "non-architectural" way. It is particularly worth mentioning that the Market Museum has provided architects with a multi-dimensional perspective on public architecture.

It is expected that more reasonable and flexible regulations in the future will allow her small-scale co-living project to be transformed into a trend in which more users can have the real experience of defining space by themselves, and that her Borderless Community concept will be realized in mass scale with even more diversifications. I also hope that architects can get some inspirations from the Market Museum project and use more diverse architectural methods in urban renewal.

July, 2022

目录
Contents

紫泥十二门无界社区
Borderless Community of Zi Ni Twelve Portals

建筑师自述 The Architect's Narration	002
六个好友的家 The Home of Six Friends	010
未来，如何共同生活 How to Live Together in the Future	106

竹丝岗无界社区
Borderless Community of Zhusigang

建筑师自述 The Architect's Narration	114
菜市场里的美术馆 A Museum in the Market	116
美术馆里的菜市场 A Market in the Museum	142

附录
Appendix

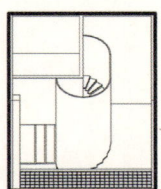

学术评论一 Academic Reviews 1	166
学术评论二 Academic Reviews 2	184
奖项·展览 Awards and Exhibitions	212
后记 Postscript	224

紫泥十二门无界社区
Borderless Community of Zi Ni Twelve Portals

建筑师自述
The Architect's Narration

米笑
Michelle Yip

扉（扉建筑、扉美术馆）合伙人
国家一级注册建筑师
英国皇家特许注册建筑师

Partner of FEI (FEI Architects, FEI Arts)
National First-class Registered Architect
Chartered Architect of RIBA (Royal Institute of British Architects)

2012年秋天，我第一次到访紫泥糖厂，被工业废墟与荒草苔原交织的景观深深吸引，萌生了"工业山水"的艺术生活园区规划构想。三年后，我终于说服一位在线办公品牌创始人租下一个旧电房，并提出共享生活空间的概念：134平方米的2层小楼可以用作办公、聚会、展览、市集、Airbnb[①]等。然而，互联网泡沫突然破裂。但我不希望这个想法只停留在图纸上，于是与六位好友共同选定了2000平方米的板材车间，用三年时间完成了"无界社区"的改造。我身边有很多"斜杠青年"，他们把工作、生活、度假、娱乐、运动融为一体。我们的设计完全打破传统建筑泾渭分明的分类，模糊的空间设定鼓励使用者自主定义功能；加厚的立面由形态各异的功能空间直接生成，动态地展示多样化的生活方式；每一套房子的花园、客厅和餐厅都可以对"街道"开放，形成更大的共享空间。通过增强互动，邻里之间可以跨越职业的界限，组织新的生产方式。

建筑本源是解决居住的问题。"无界社区"在自媒体"一条"播出后登上热搜头条，呈现出大众向往的生活方式。后疫情时代，我们将如何更好地共同生活？希望"无界社区"能为各方提供一种新的可能性。

Upon visiting the Zi Ni Sugar Factory for the first time in the autumn of 2012, I was so fascinated by the landscape of industrial ruins interwoven with wild grass and moss, and hit upon the idea of building an art and life park featuring "industrial landscape". Three years later, I finally convinced the founder of an on-line office brand to rent an abandoned power house and came up with the concept of "co-living space": a 134sqm, two-story building that could be used for office, party, exhibition, bazaar, Airbnb, etc. However, the dot-com bubble suddenly burst. But I didn't want this idea to be kept on the drawing board. So I joined six friends to pitch upon a fibreboard workshop of 2000sqm and spent three years to complete its transformation into a "Borderless Community". There are many slash youth around me, whose lifestyle integrates work, life, vacation, entertainment and sports. Our design completely breaks the clear-cut classification of conventional buildings, which adopts vague space arrangement to encourage users to customize their functions. Thickened facades are directly generated by various functional spaces, dynamically displaying diversified lifestyles. The garden, living room and dining room of each house can be opened to the "street" to form a larger shared space. By enhancing interaction, neighbors can cross professional boundaries and organize new ways of production.

The original purpose of architecture is to solve the problem of living. The "Borderless Community", after being broadcasted by the digital media "Yitiao", topped the Hot Search List, which presents a lifestyle that the public are yearning for. How can we live together in a better way in the post-pandemic era? It is hoped that the "Borderless Community" will provide a new possibility for all parties.

2022年9月
September, 2022

---

① Airbnb是AirBed and Breakfast的缩写，中文名称是爱彼迎，成立于2008年8月，总部设在美国旧金山市。Airbnb是一个旅行房屋租赁社区，用户可通过网络或手机应用程序发布、搜索房屋租赁信息，并完成在线预订。曾被《时代周刊》称为"住房中的eBay"。
Airbnb is the abbreviation of AirBed and Breakfast, whose Chinese name is 爱彼迎. Founded in August 2008 and based in San Francisco, Airbnb is a vacation rental website where users can post and search rental information, and complete booking on-line or via mobile app. *Time Magazine* once compared Airbnb to the "eBay of housing".

紫泥十二门无界社区东南立面
The southeast elevation of the Borderless Community of Zi Ni Twelve Portals

紫泥十二门无界社区东北立面
The northeast elevation of the Borderless Community of Zi Ni Twelve Portals

Dezeen建筑大奖评语：

公寓大楼通常被看作是孤立的空间，但这个项目却让我们重温那种其乐融融的邻里感觉。

Dezeen Awards Judge Comments :

Apartment buildings can be seen as isolated spaces but this helps us go back—to a neighborhood feeling where there are moments of interconnection.

WAN 世界建筑新闻奖评语：

这是一座非常美妙的共用建筑，温馨怡人，且极具质感。公寓单元的独特配置让外立面显得真实而又充满活力。

WAN Awards Judge Comments :

Welcoming, highly textural—wonderful sharing architecture. The distinctive configuration of the apartment units generate an honest and dynamic facade.

六个好友的家
The Home of Six Friends

2012年11月7日，第一次与艺术家朋友刘庆元、曾鹏到访紫泥糖厂

On November 7, 2012, I visited the Zi Ni Sugar Factory with artist friends Liu Qingyuan and Zeng Peng for the first time

群岛：为什么选择在紫泥糖厂做无界社区？

Archipelago: Why did you choose the Zi Ni Sugar Factory to build a Borderless Community?

米笑：故事要从 2012 年讲起……那年深秋，两位艺术家好友带我来到广东紫泥糖厂。这个厂区规模宏大，是曾经有卫兵把守的国家重要物资生产基地。对老番禺人来说，它是闪耀着青春荣耀的地标。2011年，厂区被列入"第三次全国文物普查重要新发现"清单，可见其历史价值。我们来到这里的时候厂区已经停产超过10年。巨大的工业废墟隐约透露出昔日机器轰隆、灯火通明的繁华景象，如今荒草萋萋、雀鸟成群，反而有种"赛博朋克"的未来感。带我来现场的艺术家们畅想着在这里建立一个后工业时代的乌托邦。我很快以"工业山水"为题做了一个艺术生活园区的改造规划方案。

Michelle Yip: The story could begin from 2012…In the late autumn of that year, two artist friends took me to Guangdong Zi Ni Sugar Factory. The factory was huge in scale and used to be an important national production base guarded by security soldiers. For many elderly people in Panyu, it is a landmark glittering with the glory of their youth. In 2011, the factory was listed in the "Important New Discoveries of the Third National Cultural Relics Census", which manifest its historical value is obvious. When we arrived, the factory had stopped production for more than 10 years. The huge industrial ruins vaguely hinted the bustling scene of roaring machines and burning lights all night in the past, but now only rampant weeds and flocks of birds could be seen, ironically emanating an ambience of Cyberpunk future. The artists who brought me to the scene wished to build a post-industrial utopia here. I quickly came up with a renovation plan to build an art and life park themed on "Industrial Landscape".

广东紫泥糖厂是中华人民共和国成立后自行设计建造的第一间大型糖厂,拥有第一条国产自动化榨糖生产线。它的建成投产,为新中国制糖工业的发展首开先河。多年来,由单一的制糖企业逐步发展为经营多种产品的大型综合企业,以日榨5000吨甘蔗制糖生产为主,兼营机制纸、水泥、酒精、饮料、商品电、纤维板、人造板等多种产品。

Guangdong Zi Ni Sugar Factory is the first domestically designed and built large-scale sugar factory since the founding of the People's Republic of China, which owns the first automatic sugar production line made in China. Its completion and commissioning marked the beginning of sugar industry development of China. Over the years, it has gradually grown from a single sugar enterprise to a large-scale comprehensive enterprise, which, besides the major output of 5000 tons of cane sugar per day, also produced paper, cement, alcohol, beverage, commercial power plant, fiberboard, wood-based panel and other products.

水泥厂
Cement plant

饮料车间蔗汁装瓶生产线
Sugarcane juice bottling production line in the beverage workshop

装卸码头
Loading dock

从1951年选址筹备建厂到1998年,因甘蔗种植面积锐减、原料短缺、制糖政策性亏损严重、资金枯竭等多种因素,于1998年9月23日作出了停止甘蔗糖生产的决定,实施分立破产,后转关闭,45年的制糖生产历史宣告结束。

Since the site selection and preparation for factory construction in 1951, after a series of setbacks including sharp decrease of sugarcane planting area, shortage of raw materials, serious losses due to sugar production policy changes and exhaustion of funds, on September 23 of 1998, the decision to stop cane sugar production was finally made, to be followed by bankruptcy and closedown of the entire enterprise. The factory's 45 years of sugar production history came to an end.

项目在粤港澳大湾区的区位，2021 年 1 月
Location of the project in the Guangdong-Hong Kong-Macao Greater Bay Area, January 2021

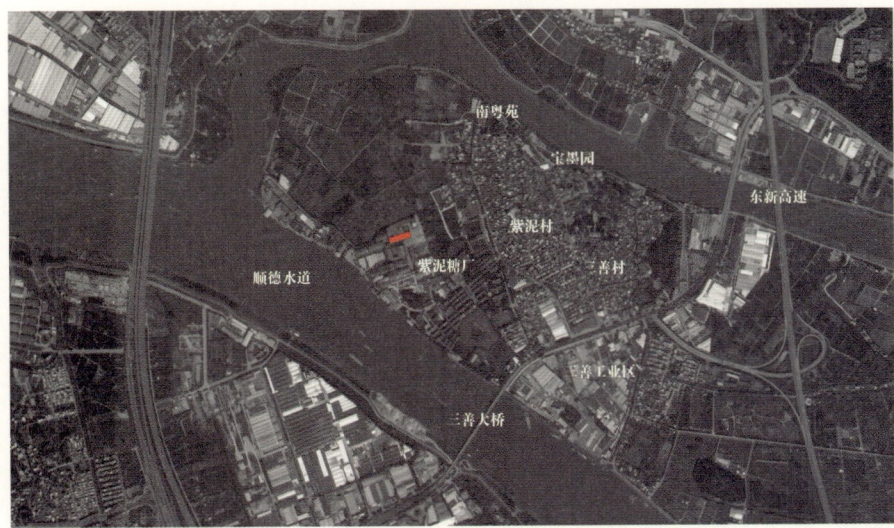

广州番禺紫泥堂①创意园卫星图，2016 年 4 月
Satellite map of Zi Ni Tang Creative Park in Panyu, Guangzhou, April 2016

---

① 紫泥堂创意园前身为原广东省最大规模蔗糖厂——广东紫泥糖厂，建于1953年。2013年紫泥堂公司成立，着手将旧厂区改造为紫泥堂创意园。
Zi Ni Tang Creative Park, formerly the largest cane sugar factory in Guangdong Province—Guangdong Zi Ni Sugar Factory, was built in 1953. In 2013, Zi Ni Tang Company was established to transform the old factory area into Zi Ni Tang Creative Park.

群岛：能不能解释一下"工业山水"的概念？

Archipelago: Could you elaborate on the concept of "industrial landscape"?

米笑：我理解中国园林其实是山水画的4D版，山水是阴阳，是平衡，是相对的。园林是中国式的乌托邦。我一直在尝试室内造园，早期的几个项目，像亿达大厦16楼、方所、星海音乐厅15周年改造，都是以抽象的山水为概念，没有真山实水，是高低、虚实的对比。眼前被荒草苔原占领的钢铁废墟令我想起艺术家杨泳梁的作品，工业化与城市化对自然的破坏是否可以利用改造的契机得以修复？我想象这些钢铁水泥架应该被丛林包裹，人与自然恢复平衡状态。

134 平方米两层高的旧电房
A deserted two-storey power house of 134sqm

Michelle Yip: To my understanding, Chinese gardens are actually a 4D-version of landscape painting. Landscape, or "mountain and water" literally in Chinese, is about Yin and Yang, balance and relativity. The Chinese Garden is a Chinese style Utopia. I have been trying to build indoor gardens. My early projects such as the 16th floor of Estate Plaza, Fangsuo Commune and the renovation of Xinghai Concert Hall at its 15th anniversary, are all based on abstract landscape concept. There is no real mountain and water, but only contrast between high and low, virtual and real. The ruins of iron and steel occupied by wild grass and moss before my eyes reminded me of the artist Yang Yongliang's work Phantom Landscape. Could the destruction of nature caused by industrialization and urbanization be repaired by taking advantage of the opportunity of transformation? I imagined that these steel and concrete frames should be wrapped in the jungle, and the balance between human and nature should be restored.

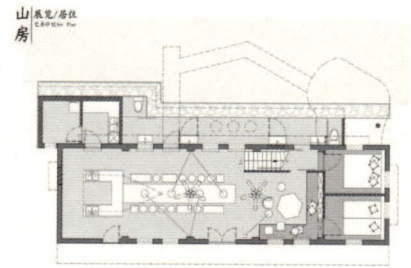 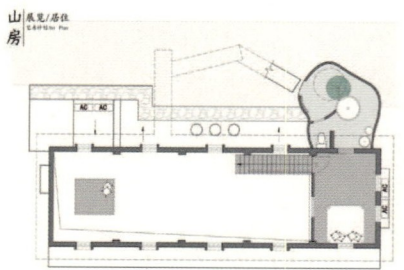 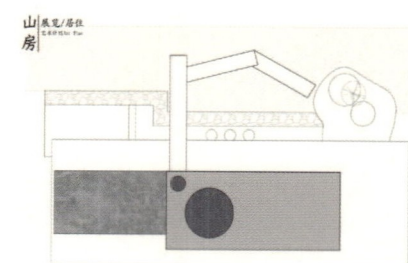

紫泥山房设计图
The design drawing of Zi Ni Mountain House

屋顶是以山丘为背景的舞台
The roof is a stage with hills as background

展厅也可以变卧室
The showroom can also be a bedroom

首层的榻榻米客房
Tatami room on the first floor

空中树屋既可以放电影,也可以是孩子们的榻榻米卧室
The treehouse in the air can be used to watch movies or as tatami bedroom for kids

一张长桌,让居住空间可以承载办公、宴会、展览等多种功能
A long table makes the living space suitable for working, banquets, exhibitions and other functions

群岛:项目为什么经历六年才完成?
Archipelago: Why did the project take six years to complete?

米笑:当时厂区的承包方没有接纳我们的规划,他们说想找个日本建筑师来设计。3年之后,第一次带我去紫泥糖厂的艺术家把工作室搬到这里,约我去参观,想起未实现的理想,我决定给自己找业主,来这里承租厂房。其中一位是杨丽萍,她受我们邀请出席云南一位著名艺术家在我们美术馆举办的展览。她去紫泥糖厂的当天就安排助手留下来选地方,并且很快就定下场地准备开工了。接着我又说服一位朋友,她是互联网社区联合办公品牌创始人,向园区租下了一个紧挨小山丘的134平米的旧电房。她说:"可不可以周一至周五是网约的联合办公空间,周末和家人来度假?"我说:"可以不止这样。"于是我提出了co-living space的设计概念:可以工作,可以开会,可以展销,可以Airbnb,可以开派对……工作、居住、展览三不误。这个名叫"紫泥山房"的就是"无界社区"前传"无界的家":一个开放厨房加一条大长桌成为空间主角,上面吊的树屋既可以作为榻榻米房又可以放电影。特制的床随时可以翻起变展板,屋顶甚至可以变剧场……

Michelle Yip: The contractor of the factory did not accept our plan at that time. They said they wanted to find a Japanese architect to design it. Three years later, the artist who accompanied me for the first visit moved his studio here and asked me to visit it again. Remembering my aborted dream, I decided to look for someone myself who would rent a workshop here. One of the potential tenants I approached was Yang Liping, who happened to be invited by us to attend an exhibition by a famous artist from Yunnan in our museum. On the same day she visited the factory, and asked her assistant to stay and pick a site. In early 2016, the site was ready for construction. Then I persuaded another friend, the founder of an Internet community co-working brand, to rent a 134sqm deserted power house in the factory, which is close to a hill. She asked: "Can I have a co-working space from Monday to Friday that can be reserved on-line and also come over with my family to spend weekends?" I answered: "It can be more than that." So I put forward the "co-living space" concept: a place for people to work, have meetings, host exhibitions and bazaars, list on Airbnb, and throw parties, etc. The project named "Zi Ni Mountain House" is the prequel of "Borderless Community", the "Borderless Home": an open kitchen plus a long table becomes the main character of the space; the tree house hanging above can be used as tatami room and home cinema; the special bed can be turned up at any time to change into exhibition board; the roof can even be turned into a theatre…

但2015年底,她没有找到新的投资人,便结束了联合办公的创业路。然而我们心中的蓝图更清晰了,更加渴望能够把想法实现。

But at the end of 2015, she failed to find new investors and closed her co-working business. Nevertheless, the vision in our heart has become clearer and we are more eager to realize our ideas.

与艺术家宋冬一起踏勘现场,2016年8月
Inspecting the site with artist Song Dong in August, 2016

我拿着这个方案向身边的朋友"兜售"。他们大多是创意工作者,看了方案都无比激动,纷纷要求一起做联合办公室。我带着朋友们多次到厂区寻找合适的厂房。最开始选的是靠近沙湾水道的废弃水泥厂,这里还有专用码头。2015年底我去探访当代艺术家宋冬的工作室,他们家院子有个"白做园",是用装修剩下的淤泥堆砌的,就成了作品。这个作品后来在世界很多城市做过。我想水泥厂那么多废水泥渣,正好用来堆成景观山水,就像城市规划,先造景,围着"景观绿地"再造房。2016年夏天我邀请宋冬老师来看现场,同时也请何志森(Jason)就水泥厂做名为"废墟里的桃花源"的mapping工作坊。随后宋冬参观扉艺廊的时候提出了"无界的墙"的想法,于是有了扉美术馆2017年无界系列的开启,何志森也成了我们美术馆馆长。

何志森踏勘现场,2016年9月
Jason Zhisen Ho inspecting the site in September, 2016

I took this plan to "sell" it to my friends around me, most of whom were in creative industry. They got very excited about the plan and were eager to join the co-working project. So I took my friends to the factory several times to look for suitable workshop building. Our first choice was the abandoned cement workshop near Shawan waterway, which has its own wharf. At the end of 2015, I paid a visit to the studio of contemporary artist Song Dong. There was a Doing Nothing Garden in the yard, which is made of piles of silt left over from decoration. This work made from waste was later re-created in many cities around the world. I hit upon the idea that since the cement plant had so much sewage sludge, they could just be piled up to make landscape. Like urban planning, we can first build landscape, and then rebuild the house around the "green landscape". In the summer of 2016, I invited Mr. Song Dong to inspect the site, and also invited Jason Zhisen Ho to do a mapping workshop named "Peach Blossom Land in the Ruins" in the cement workshop. Later, when Song Dong visited FEI Gallery(predecessor of FEI Arts Museum), he put forward the idea of Borderless Wall and hence the launch of FEI Arts Museum's Borderless Series 2017. Since then Jason has become the curator of our museum.

可是由于水电设施不完善,无法对水泥厂进行改造,我们最后选定了位于厂区中部的板材车间,原因是这是最后一批建成的厂房之一,外观毫无特色,且附

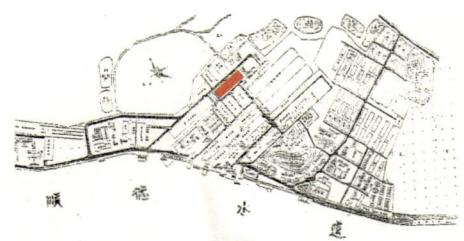

紫泥十二门位于糖厂西侧中部，全长110米
Zi Ni Twelve Portals is located in the middle of the west side of Sugar Factory, with a total length of 110m

近还有同样的一座建筑。同时，这里没有什么景观，业主愿意低价出租。

However, owing to the inadequate water and electricity facilities, the cement plant couldn't be renovated. We finally picked a fiberboard workshop in the middle of the factory. Being among the latest built workshops, it was featureless and there was a similar one in the vicinity. Moreover, due to the lack of scenery nearby, the owner was willing to rent it out at a low price.

经过大半年的选址、设计，终于在2016年国庆动工了。我们把兼容办公与住宿的co-living概念发展为共同生活、共同创造的"无界社区"。其中一位"村民"bEn将这里命名叫"紫泥十二门"——从前有座山，山上面住着12个神仙……

After more than half a year spent on site selection and design, the construction finally started during National Day holiday in October, 2016. We developed the co-living concept, which combines work and life, into "Borderless Community" featuring "working and living together". One of the "villagers", bEn, named this place "Zi Ni Twelve Portals"—once upon a time, there was a mountain with 12 immortals living in it...

原无胶纤维板厂东立面
East elevation of the original fiberboard workshop

群岛：不是说六个好友吗？

Archipelago: Didn't you say six friends?

米笑：12也是虚指，就是多种多样。实际比较多参加设计讨论的是其中2位，都是需要家和工作室在一起的。

Michelle Yip: 12 also has a virtual sense, which means "variety". In fact, two of the friends participated in the design discussion more often, who want to combine home and studio.

群岛：多样性从建成效果是看出来了，但他们提的需求有什么共同之处呢？

Archipelago: The diversity is evident as shown by the completed house, but do they have any demands in common?

米笑：一是要花园，所有事情都想在花园里完成，喝茶、吃饭、泡澡，甚至午睡……这也跟我原本的"工业山水"提案相符。所以现在这个房子看起来"满身破洞"就是房间穿插在花园中的结果。二是要灵活可变，一室多用。大家讨论的时候提出过像古罗马那样泡澡时开会议事的场景。设计中呈现的不是多人场景，而是最小的阁楼套间的浴池，也可以做读书聊天的角落或者儿童乐园。

Michelle Yip: Firstly, they all want a garden and have everything done in the garden like drinking, eating, bathing, and even napping...This happens to be in line with my original "industrial landscape" proposal. So now the house looks like it's "full of holes", which is the result of multiple rooms interspersed around gardens. Secondly, it should be flexible and multipurpose. During our discussion, we had imagined a scene of having meetings in the bath like in ancient Rome. What the design finally presented is not a multi-person setting, but a bath in the smallest attic suite, which could serve as both reading and chatting corner and playground for kids.

群岛：花6年完成项目，为什么最后没有搬进去真正"共同生活"？

Archipelago: Why didn't you finally move into the house that took 6 years to complete and really "live together"？

米笑：政策原因。工业厂房不能改为居住用房。两位铁杆支持者是一定要工作室跟住宅结合为一体的，没办法就退出了。其中一位资金比较宽裕的就接着投入把项目完成了。

Michelle Yip: It's due to policy reason. Industrial properties cannot be converted into residential buildings. The two die-hard supporters must combine studio with home, so they had no choice but to quit. One of them who is better-funded went on to complete the project.

群岛：没有成为真正的社区，这个项目有何意义？
Archipelago: What's the meaning of the project, as it fails to be a real community?

米笑：车展、航空展都有展出未投产的概念车、未来机型。紫泥十二门就是这种"未来款"。造出来了，可以体验了，有样版了，才有机会讨论量产的可能性。这个意义就是打样。

Michelle Yip: There are concept cars and future models on display at auto shows and air shows, which have not yet been put into production. Zi Ni Twelve Portals is exactly this kind of "future style". Once the model is made and can be experienced, there would be the opportunity to discuss the possibility of mass production. This is the meaning of the project.

群岛：现在已经是后疫情时代，这个10年前的构想、6年前的设计能符合未来的需求吗？
Archipelago: Now in the post-pandemic era, can the concept conceived 10 years ago and the design made 6 years ago meet the needs of future?

米笑：恰恰是经历疫情，我们发现原本为创意工作者设计的在家工作、社交、娱乐、运动、带娃这种无界生活方式，在疫情后变成多数人的需求。而且就算是极端的社区隔离状态，在这里，邻居之间依然能够互动，足不出户也可以互相招呼问候，真正做到"隔而不离"。其中大拖小的户型，原本小户是作Airbnb出租，疫情下多了个功能——作为社区隔离空间。无界社区不仅仅是户内设计可以灵活适应不同的功能需求，更重要的是构建共同生活的积极邻里空间，这恰恰是后疫情时代最需要的。

Michelle Yip: It is precisely through the epidemic that we realize that the borderless lifestyle originally designed for creative workers to work, socialize, entertain, exercise and raise kids at home, has become the need of most people after the pandemic. And even in the extreme state of community quarantine, here, neighbors can still interact with each other, greet each other without leaving home, and thus are never really separated from each other. The suite model with a big flat and a small flat, originally to be rented as Airbnb, now acquires a new function druing the pandemic, i.e., serves as community quarantine space. The Borderless Community not only has an interior design that can flexibly adapt to a variety of functional demands, but more importantly, it builds a positive neighborhood space for co-living, which is exactly most needed in the post-pandemic era.

与六个好友一起选场地盖房子
Joining Six Friends to Look for Suitable Site to Build a House Together

经过差不多一年的现场勘察、工作坊研讨、选址、设计讨论,终于在 2016 年初选定在纤维板车间一起建造"无界社区"。
After almost a year of on-site investigation, workshops discussions, site selection and design discussions, the decision was finally made to build a "Borderless Community" in the fiberboard workshop in early 2016.

① 2012 年冬,首次到访紫泥糖厂园区
  The first visit to Zi Ni Sugar Factory park in the winter of 2012

② 2015 年秋,与一位互联网社区联合办公品牌创始人到访园区,选定小电房
  In the autumn of 2015, we accompanied the founder of a coworking brand in the internet community to visit the park and decided on the small power house

③ 2015 年 10 月,水泥厂
  Cement plant, October 2015

④ 煤仓,如今已改为泳池
  Coal bunker, converted into swimming pool now

⑤ 2016 年春节,巴瓦之行讨论无界社区雏形
  The Bawa trip during spring festival of 2016, to discuss the embryonic form of Borderless Community

⑥ 何志森在无界社区的前奏——"废墟里的桃花源"工作坊现场
  Jason Zhisen Ho at the site of the "Peach Blossom Land in the Ruins" workshop — the prelude of Borderless Community

⑦⑧ "废墟里的桃花源"工作坊总结分享
  Summary and sharing of "Peach Blossom Land in the Ruins" workshop

⑤ ⑥ ⑦

⑬ ⑭ ⑮

⑨ 园区内调研
Making research in the park

⑩ 第一次方案讨论
The first discussion on the plan

⑪ 艺术家冯峰、卢麃麃在现场讨论
Artists Feng Feng and Lu Biaobiao in discussions on the site

⑫ 艺术家宋冬在现场
Artist Song Dong on the site

⑬ 在扉建筑工作室讨论无界社区方案
Discussing about the Borderless Community plan at FEI Architects studio

⑭ 与艺术家李伟斌（bEn）、张小川讨论方案
Discussing the plan with artists bEn Li and Zhang Xiaochuan

⑮ 与陶艺家五楼讨论方案
Discussing the plan with ceramic artist Wulou

21

2015 年深冬首次到纤维板车间现场
Visiting the fiberboard workshop for the first time in the late winter of 2015

在房子里盖房子的概念模型
The conceptual model of building houses within a house

紫泥十二门最终模型
The final model of Zi Ni Twelve Portals

原无胶纤维板厂（摄于 2016 年 2 月）
The original fiberboard workshop (shot in February, 2016)

南立面效果图 (绘制于 2017 年 1 月)
South elevation rendering (drawn in January, 2017)

六个好友的家
The Home of Six Friends

6 年之后，我们终于把房子盖好了
After 6 years, we finally completed the building

2018年中，车间的机电塔楼基本完成改造。首先入驻的是一窝小鸟，大家都很欢欣，觉得紫泥十二门就是风水宝地。
In mid-2018, transformation of the electromechanical tower of the workshop was basically completed. The first "resident" was a nest of birds, which made everyone so happy and think Zi Ni Twelve Portals was on a blessed land.

同事在一株琴叶榕发现了无界社区的第一家"住户"
The first "resident" to settle down in the Borderless Community was found in a fiddle leaf fig by our colleagues

一只麻雀妈妈在这里筑巢生下小宝宝
A sparrow nested here and gave birth to her babies

15米×18米×13.2米的机电塔楼内植入了六套大小不一的房子，反映了身边创意人群对家的美好想象，也同市面流行的一些房地产户型有对照关系。

塔楼的表皮加厚成空间，直接反映每个户型的真实功能组成。我们没有设计立面，是使用者的需求创造了建筑的表皮。

塔楼容纳大小六套单元。先说其中三个小单元，如何让人在有限的空间过得活色生香。

Six houses of different sizes are implanted in the electromechanical tower of 15m×18m×13.2m, which reflects the imagination of the creative people around me for their dream home, and makes contrast to some popular house types in the market.

The exterior of the building is thickened to make space to directly reflect configuration of the real functions of each home. We did not design the facade; it was the needs of the users generated it.

The tower accommodates six units of various sizes. Firstly, let's see how the three small units enable people to live a colorful life in a limited space.

永不落幕的生活剧场
The never-ending theatre of life

飘窗的实验
An Experiment with the Bay Window

西神的家：35 平方米有天池的房子
Season's home: A 35sqm house with "heaven lake"

职业：初出茅庐的策展小白
Occupation: A beginner engaged in curation

斜杠爱好：二手旧物收藏、收养流浪动物
Hobbies: Collecting second-hand items; adopting stray animals

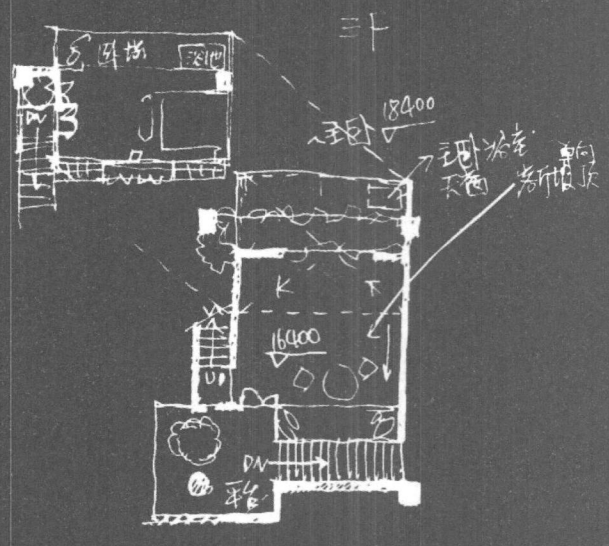

Loft 公寓是房地产市场上特别受年轻人欢迎的产品。一般都是下面为客厅，搭个小阁楼做卧室的很雷同的设计。我想为身边的"90 后"量身定做一个五脏俱全的家，从单身到二人世界到生儿育女都能在这个 4.2 米高、35 平方米大的蜗居其乐融融。故事的原型是我们美术馆当时的执行总监，她从实习生开始就在"扉"工作，前后近 10 年。她非常爱养猫，喜欢在家做饭待客，且有无数有趣男女好友的潮汕女生，所以就有了这个厨房面向田野，大桌子而非沙发掌控全局的平面。卧室被压缩到一个小角落吊起来，这个想法源于前传"紫泥山房"的树屋，对于房地产"必杀技"飘窗，我在这个房子也做了突破性实验。一个是客厅的飘窗，伸向街道，变成展示空间。这是对十几年前开在居民楼的广州第一家设计买手店 Benshop 的回忆。另外一个是向室内加深变成小阳台。贴上黑白格子马赛克，既可以种植，又可以做浴池，还可以给宠物安家，最后若是有孩子，波波池变为孩子的乐园。因为不想做一个无聊的楼梯，所以高差分为三段，首段消化 45 厘米，是个平台，朋友来可以借宿，也可以是猫窝；第二段 1.2 米高差用 300 毫米×300 毫米的盒子做楼梯，搭出一个陈列空间，随时可以在家办小展览，例如陶艺、潮玩；最后是连接卧室和浴池的"桥"，落下的卷帘正好是投影幕，可以"猫"在阁楼看电影，尺寸也刚好是一张单人床，好客的主人可以同时招待更多的朋友。

Loft Apartment is a product particularly popular with young people in the real estate market. Such apartments all have very similar design usually consisting of a sitting room below and a small attic as bedroom. I want to tailor a home for the post-90s generation around me, which could accommodate various functions for happy family life in a 4.2m high, 35sqm humble abode in different stages ranging from single, couple to family with baby. The prototype of the story is the Executive Director of FEI Gallery at that time, who had worked with FEI for nearly 10 years since her internship. As a girl from Chaoshan, she loves cats and cooking, has lots of interesting friends of both genders and enjoys entertaining guests at home. So she has a kitchen facing the field and a large table rather than a sofa to dominate the whole floor plan; moreover, the bedroom was "squeezed" to a small corner and "hung up", which was inspired by the tree house of the previous Zi Ni Mountain House. I also made a breakthrough experiment with the house in its bay window design, which has always been designer's trump card. For example, the bay window of the living room is extended to the street and becomes a display space. It reminds people of Benshop, the first design buyer shop opened in residential district in Guangzhou more than a decade ago. Another bay window is turned into a small balcony by deepening the interior. Pasted with black and white lattice mosaic, it can be flowerbed, bathtub, home for cats and even ball pond for kids. Furthermore, instead of making a boring staircase, the height difference is divided into three sections. The first section of 45cm is a platform for friends to stay overnight or serve as cat house; The second section of 1.2m is a staircase composed of 300mm×300mm boxes, which can be set up as display space at any time to host small exhibitions at home for products like pottery and trendy crafts; Finally, there is a "bridge" connecting the bedroom and the bath, which is just the size of a single bed, so that the hospitable hostess can accommodate more friends at the same time, and the falling curtain can be projection screen for one to crouch in the attic to watch movies.

邻里关系图
Neighborhood Relations Diagram

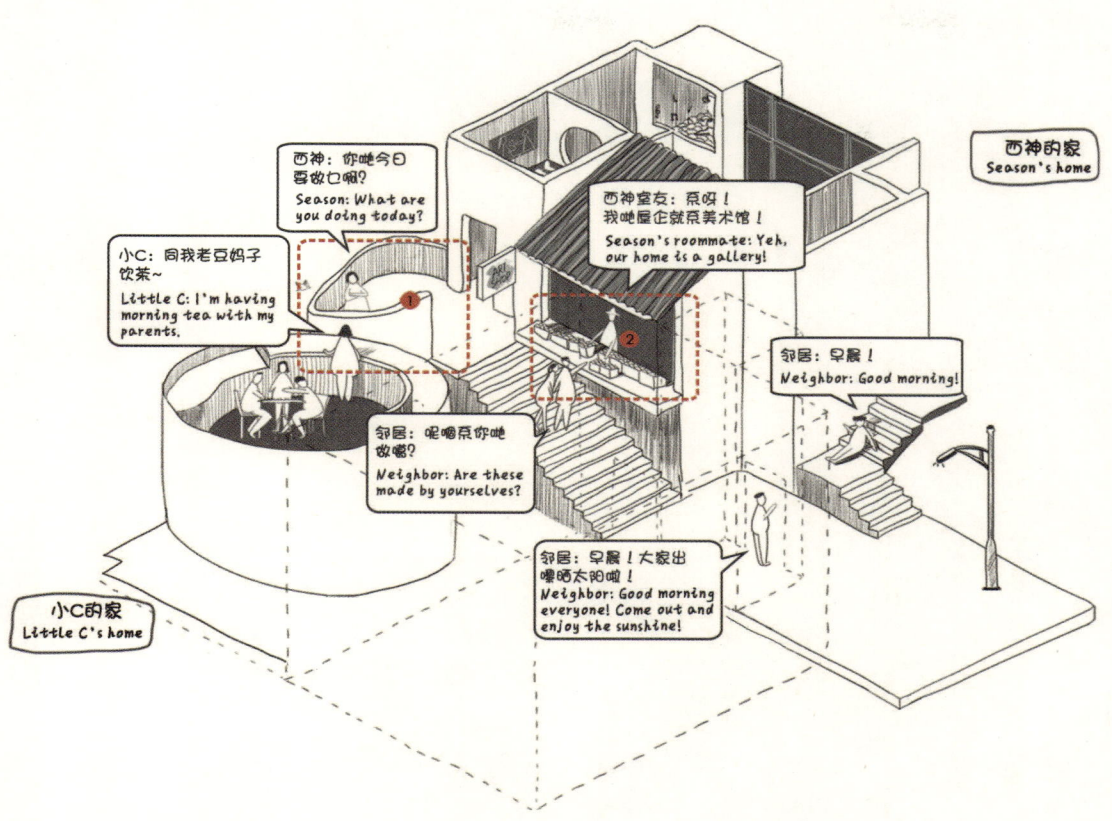

① 错位露台之间形成的上下对望空间
Deliberately located balconies allow neighbors to see each other from up or down

② 兼顾展示功能的飘窗
Bay window/showcase

透过卧室拱门看多用泡池
Looking through the bedroom arch at the multi-purpose ball pool

聊天、喝茶
Chatting, drinking tea

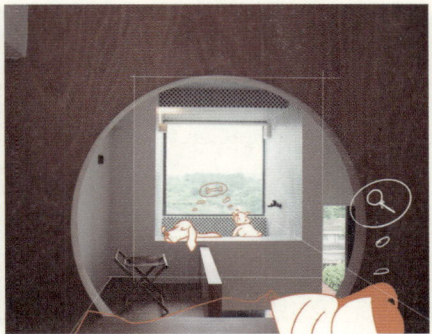
人宠空间
Space for people and pets

儿童波波池
Kids' bubble tub

泡澡
Bubble bath

花园种植
Gardening

瑜伽
Yoga

卧榻
Couch

摄影基地
Photography base

家庭电影院
Home cinema

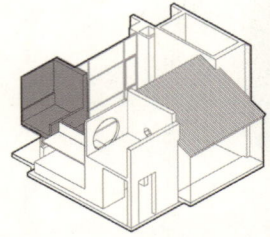
泡池在西神家的空间位置图
The tub's location in Season's home

35

飘窗也可以是派对吧
The bay window can also be a party bar

卧榻
Couch

店铺
Shop

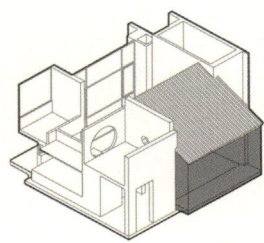
飘窗在西神家的空间位置图
The bay window's location in Season's home

①

②

③

④

⑤

⑥

⑦

⑧

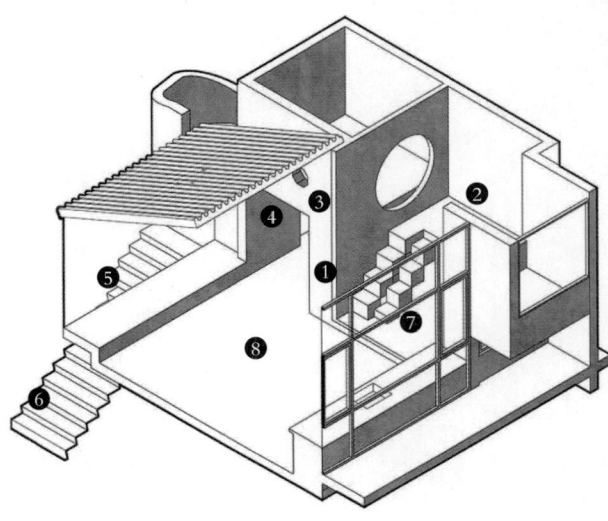

西神的家空间构成
Space composition of Season's home

① 公寓全景
Panorama of the apartment

② 从卧室俯看天池与厨房、工作区
Overlooking "heaven lake", kitchen and studio from the bedroom

③ 室内的坡屋顶带出小空间的温馨感
The indoor sloped roof accentuates the coziness of small space

④ 呼应天池的黑白创作的艺术品定义了玄关
The black and white artwork specially created to echo "heaven lake", defines the hallway

⑤ 夕阳下的楼梯间
The staircase under the sunset

⑥ 西神家门前的入户楼梯
The entry stairs in front of Season's home

⑦ 平台可以开微型展览,坐在台阶喝酒看电影也不错
The small terrace for mini exhibitions with steps that can be sat on while drinking or watching movies

⑧ 卫浴空间把盥洗台敞开,扩大丰富了客厅的空间感
The washstand of the toilet is open towards the outside to enhance the richness of the living room

可以和邻居打招呼的阳台
The balcony where one can say hello to neighbors

都市农场
Urban Farm

娟姐的家：80 平方米有廊的房子
Sister Juan's home: An 80sqm house with veranda

职业：家族财富管理顾问
Occupation: Family wealth management consultant

斜杠爱好：城市农夫
Hobbies: Urban farmer

经过使用者的长年经营，老城区的阳台透露出丰富的个体信息。当一个房子的立面完全是阳台，会呈现出怎样的生活状态？身边的朋友关注可持续发展问题的特别多，其中一位是家族财富管理的专业人士，她的业余爱好是推广都市阳台农场，还跟我们美术馆合作过社区种植公益课。我打算为她设计一个房子，厨房就对着种满蔬菜和香料的花园。房子带有 11 米的长玻璃屋阳台，可以是一个都市农场，也可以是艺术家、设计师的展厅，人们在楼下的街道就可以看到他们的作品展。在现场，我们制作了一个名为"In Art We Trust"的灯光装置。

After so many years of operation, the verandas in the old downtown areas reveal a lot of personal information of their users. If the whole facade of a house is just a veranda, what kind of state of life will it present? There are quite a few friends around me who pay special attention to sustainable development issues. One of them is a professional in family wealth management whose hobby is to promote urban veranda farms. She once cooperated with our art museum in public welfare courses of community planting. I'm going to design a house for her, with a kitchen facing a garden full of vegetables and spices. The house with 11m long veranda/glass room, can be a city farm, or an exhibition hall for artists and designers, whose works can be seen from the street downstairs. On the spot, we made a light installation named "In Art We Trust".

邻里关系图
Neighborhood Relations Diagram

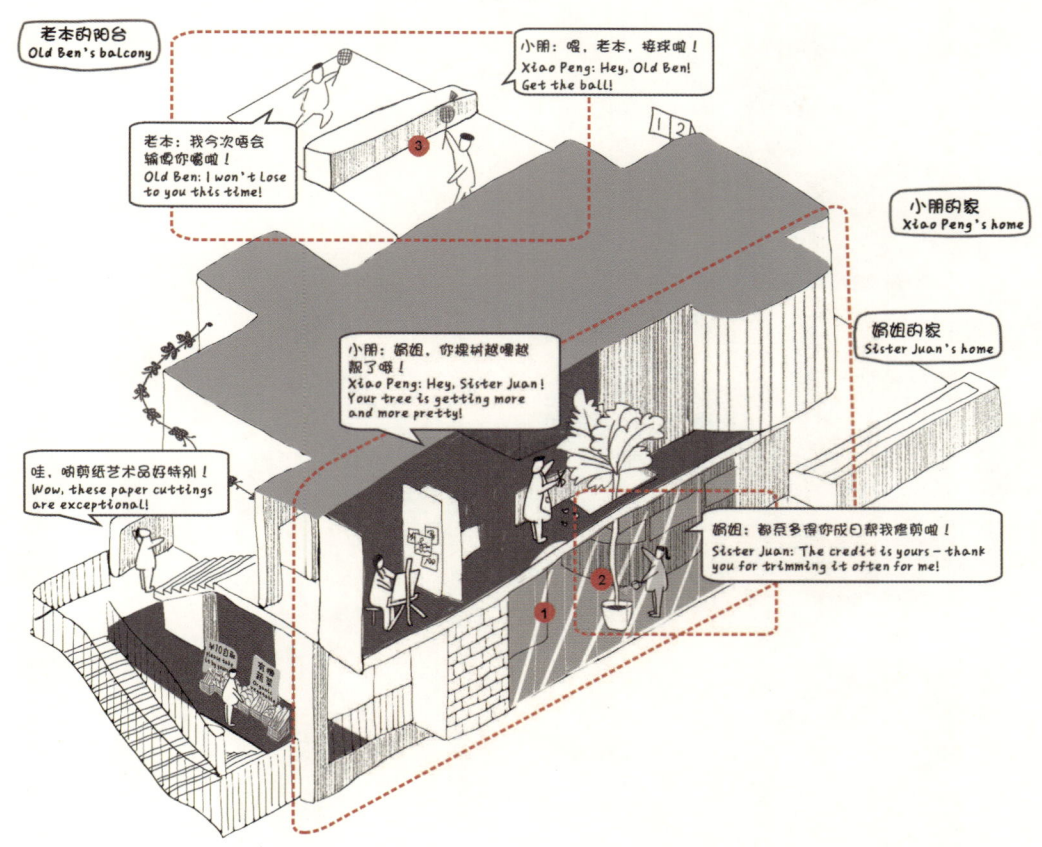

① 夜幕降临后的彩色玻璃长廊呈现出不同功能
The stained-glass corridor presenting different functions after nightfall

② 连接厨房的温室菜园
The greenhouse vegetable garden connected with the kitchen

③ 可以与邻居打球的露台
The balcony where one can play ball with the neighbor

与邻居共享的玻璃长廊
Glass veranda shared with neighbors

展厅
Exhibition hall

菜园
Vegetable garden

加建大楼梯变复式大套
Duplex suite with added staircase

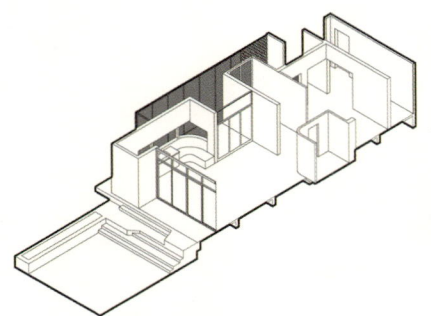

玻璃长廊在娟姐家的空间位置图
The glass veranda's location at Sister Juan's home

①

②

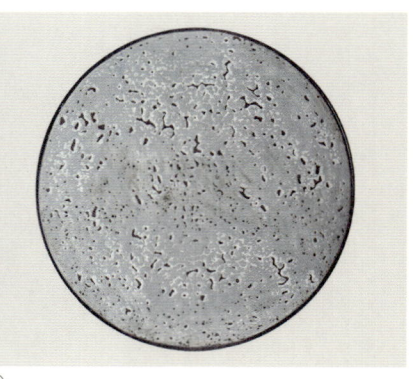
③

④

⑤

⑥

⑦

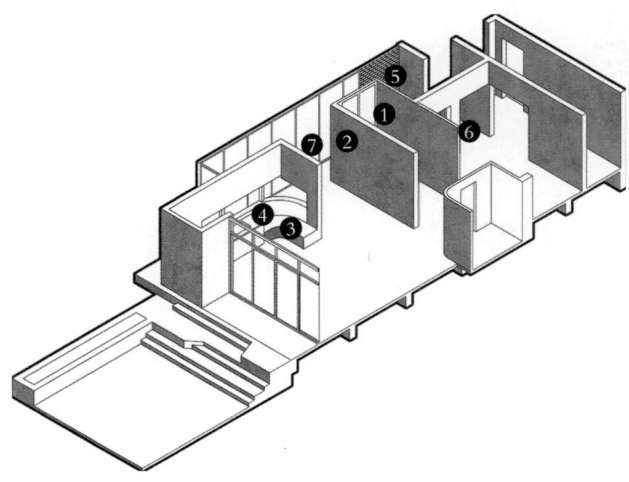

娟姐的家空间构成
Space composition of Sister Juan's home

① 面向玻璃长廊的茶室，也可以用作卧室
The tea room facing the long glass veranda can also be used as bedroom

② 为玻璃展厅创作的艺术品
The artwork created for the glass exhibition hall

③ 自创陶瓷板餐桌桌面
An originally created ceramic dinner table top

④ 从灶台延伸到座椅，区分出早餐区
Extending from stove to seats with distinguished breakfast area

⑤ 花园浴室
Bathroom in the garden

⑥ 卧室角落
Corner of the bedroom

⑦ 可以与楼上邻居打招呼的长廊菜园
Long veranda with planted vegetables where one could say hello to the neighbors upstairs

超级阳台的 N 种打开方式
Infinite Ways to Open a "Super-Balcony"

小朋的家：80 平方米有亭子的房子
Xiao Peng's home: An 80 sqm house with pavilion

职业：生活杂志编辑
Occupation: Life magazine editor

斜杠爱好：养盆栽、做手工陶艺
Hobbies: Growing potted plants, pottery hand-making

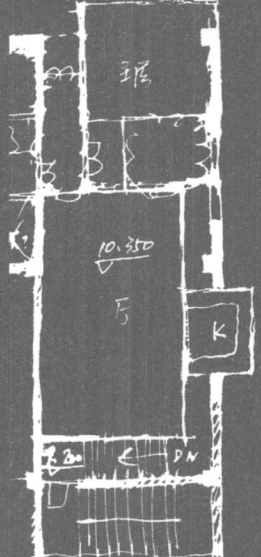

跟身边朋友聊他们向往的房子的时候，花园（阳台）似乎是同一个梦想。拿房子的一半出来做花园如何？通过设身处地的思考后，决定在花园里盖个亭子间，可开可合，可以向客厅打开扩展为书房，向花园打开扩展为茶室，关闭就是客房。以同样的开合方式处理卧室与附设全天候小阳台的关系：打开可以是化妆间或收藏心头好的房间，关闭可以是阳光书房、宠物乐园。事实上，可开可合的大进深阳台极大地丰富了全天候的气候适应性生活方式。

When talking to friends about their dream house, garden (balcony) seems to be their common dream. How about taking half of the house to make a garden? After some deliberate consideration by putting myself in the shoes of the homeowner, I decide to build a pavilion in the garden, which can be open or closed. Being open to the living room, it is a study; being open to the garden, it is a tearoom; and being closed, it is a guestroom. The relationship between the bedroom and the all-weather small balcony is treated in the same way via a switch: in the open mode, it can be makeup room or collection room; in the closed mode, it can be a sunny study or pet's playground. In fact, such a big deep balcony with open and closed modes greatly enriches the versatile lifestyle adaptable to all climates and weathers.

邻里关系图
Neighborhood Relations Diagram

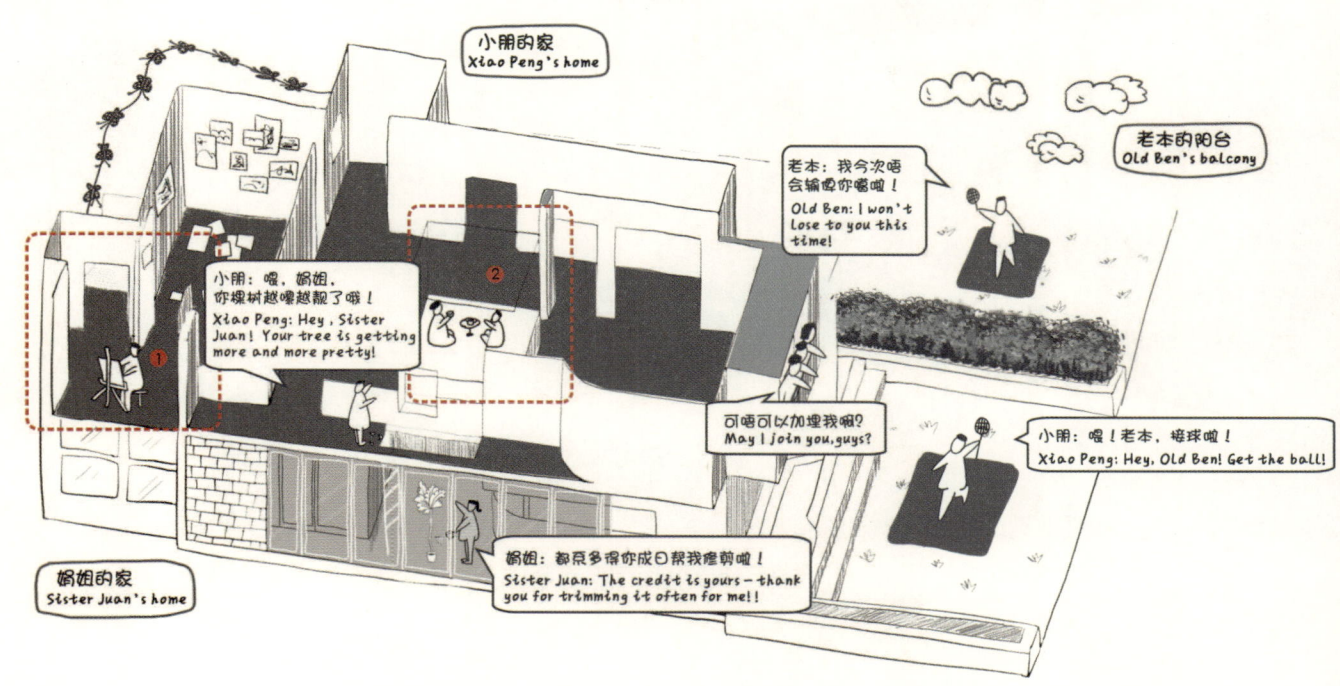

① 与卧室相连、可开可合的内阳台
The interior balcony connected with the bedroom, which can be opened and closed

② 晨间的茶亭
The tea pavilion in the morning

扩展"门"的概念,使其成为可以移动的"墙",开合之间延展卧室的多种使用可能
Expanding the concept of door to make it a movable wall, the bedroom's multi-functions become possible via the door's opening and closing

艺术家画廊
The artist's gallery

衣橱
The wardrobe

人宠空间
Space for people and pets

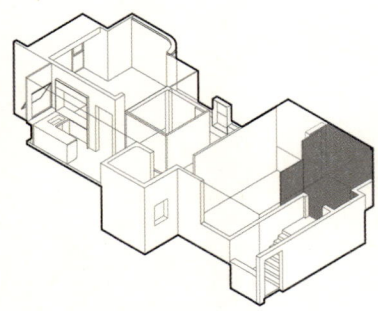

内阳台在小朋家的空间位置图
Interior balcony's location in Xiao Peng's home

嵌入边界的岛台,打开时是渗透到客厅的厨艺课堂,关闭时是孩子的补习黑板
The "island platform" embedded in the border could serve for cooking class that permeates into the living room when it's opened; when it's closed, it could be a blackboard for kids' extracurricular classes

上厨艺课
A cooking class

开会
A meeting

孩子的补习课堂
A cram course for kids

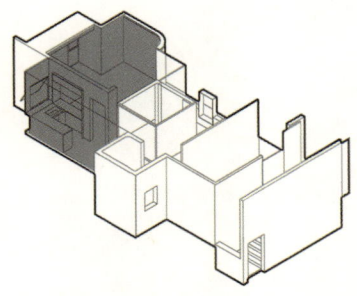

吧台在小朋家的空间位置图
Bar's location in Xiao Peng's home

① ② ③ ④ ⑤ ⑥ ⑦ ⑧ ⑨

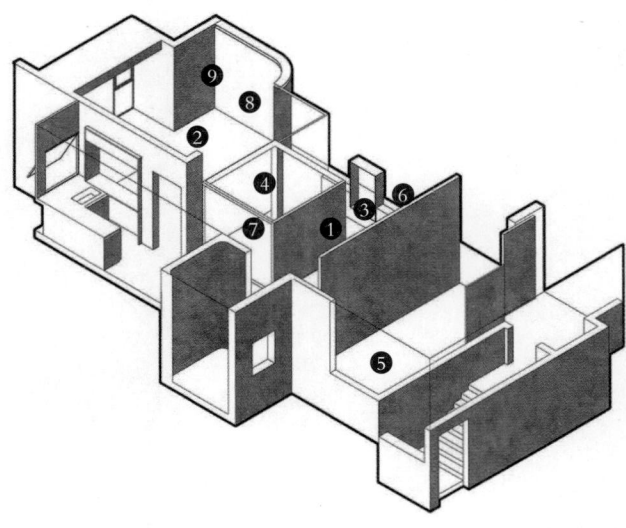

小朋的家空间构成
Space composition of Xiao Peng's home

① 为大进深敞厅创作的灯光装置"声波"
The lighting device "Sound Wave" created for the deep open hall

② 自创陶瓷板八仙桌桌面
The originally designed ceramic slab old-fashioned square table top

③ 陶艺工作室 / 茶室
Pottery studio/Tea room

④ 可以兼做客房的半透明茶亭
Translucent tea pavilion that can also serve as guestroom

⑤ 卧室一角
A corner of the bedroom

⑥ 阳台 / 晾坯空间
Balcony/Airing Space

⑦ 茶室也可以变身展厅
The teahouse can become an exhibition hall

⑧ 天光壁龛适合展示自制陶艺
The skylight niche is fit for displaying handmade pottery works

⑨ 带天窗的读书角
The reading corner with skylight

邻里之间的共享空间
The space shared by neighbors

茶亭也是放映空间
The tea pavilion can be a projection booth

再说说另外三套复式户型。

大平层还是小复式？年轻人肯定热衷于跑上跑下，所以在这里我们尝试了三种复式户型。跟房地产项目不同，这三套200多平方米的房子都是"楼中楼"，有大家，也有小家。设计灵感源于我小时候常常到西关走亲戚。他们住的竹筒楼（长屋）是几房人住的，打开房间的窗透过小天井能看到对面的房，关上窗后房间就自有天地。这种开合也源于古村落三间两廊的布局，当大家都打开门，其实一条村就是一个大房子，就是一个大家。通过开合调节居住者的心理距离，这与现在房地产的模式非常不一样。我尝试在普通的三房两厅做出这种开合关系，"楼中楼"就是一套大房子，由一大一小两套房子组合而成，可分可合。最后这个概念也从几个复式单元扩展到整个项目，变成"无界社区"。

Secondly, let's talk about another three duplexes.

Would you prefer big flat or small duplex? Young people are definitely more enthusiastic about running up and down, so here we attempted to design three duplexes. Different from normal residential projects, the three houses of more than 200sqm each are all "building in the building" accommodating both big and small families. The design inspiration comes from my childhood experience of visiting relatives living in Xiguan. The "bamboo tube building"(long house) they lived in used to be inhabited by several families, and looking from the room's windows, one could see the room on the other side through the small patio. When the windows are closed, the room is a world of its own. Such layout stems from the ancient village featuring three rooms with two corridors. When everybody opens the door, the whole village is actually a big house and a big family. This kind of open and closed modes represents adjustable psychological distance, and is very different from the current real estate model. I want to create such relationship with open and closed modes in the common suite with three rooms and two halls; the "building in the building" means a complex house comprised of a big house and a small house, which can both be divided and combined. This concept expands from several duplex units to the whole project and eventually becomes "Borderless Community".

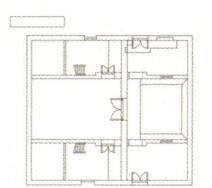 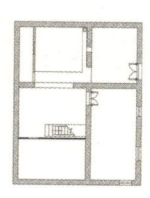 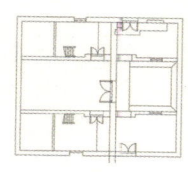 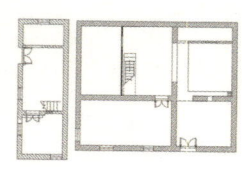

紫泥十二门无界社区东立面
East elevation of the Borderless Community of Zi Ni Twelve Portals

养老计划
Retirement Plan

仙帝的家：230 平方米有桥的房子
Cindy's home: A 230sqm house with bridge

职业：专栏作家
Occupation: Columnist

斜杠爱好：网上开直播课教咖啡烘焙、精油控
Hobbies: Teaching coffee roasting on-line; essential oil enthusiast

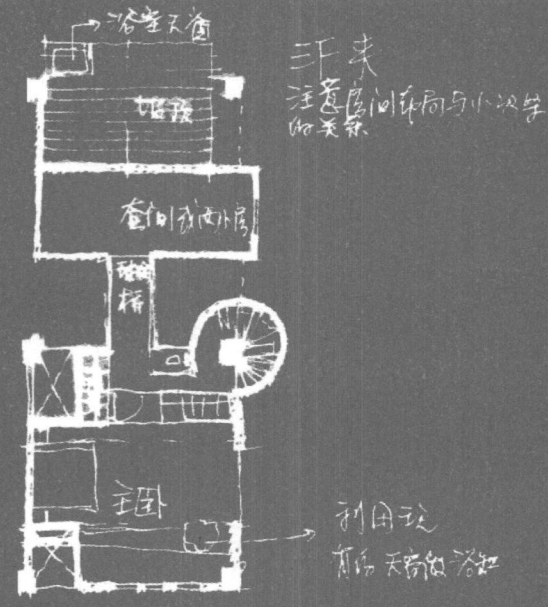

大多数人可能首先被这个有圆形窗的书房吸引，其实这套房子构思的是一个养老计划。文艺青年的梦想大概离不开拥有一家咖啡店或者一个爱彼迎（Airbnb）。去新西兰和日本旅行的时候住了好几家 Airbnb，是真的跟主人住同一屋檐下，早餐聊聊天就能很好地了解当地的经济、文化、民俗，跟国内的民宿不一样。有没有可能设计一种户型，有咖啡，有 Airbnb，一次过满足文青的全部愿望？我把房地产比较常见的入户带一个"老人套房"的户型改了一下，用一个垂直花园分隔独立小套房与一个两房两厅的大套。厨房做成面向花园的开放式。这是一个全生命周期的设计：老人来带孩子的时候可以有独立的生活空间，厨房餐厅是一家人共聚天伦的地方。孩子长大了，小套变婚房，两代人依然可以各有空间。等小两口再生儿育女搬出去，小套又可以做 Airbnb，或者出租给城市白领，开放厨房变咖啡店。这样，老人可以有了新的伙伴以及额外的养老收入。这个 10 平方米的小花园增加了房子的公共与私密之间的层次关系，带来更多可能性。

Most people may first be attracted by the study with round windows. In fact, the concept of this house is a retirement plan. It is the dream of most "wenqing"(cultured youth) to own a coffeeshop or an Airbnb. I stayed in several Airbnbs during my trip to New Zealand and Japan, and really lived under the same roof with the hosts. I could get a good understanding of the local economy, culture and folklore by chatting with them at breakfast, which is different from the domestic homestay. Is it possible to design a house with coffeeshop and Airbnb to meet all wenqing's wishes at one time? Based on the common house plan with a "suite for the elderly", I make some changes and use a vertical garden to separate the independent small suite from the large one with two rooms and two halls. The kitchen is open to the garden. This is a design for the full life cycle: when the elderly parents join the family to take care of their grandchildren, they can have an independent living space and the kitchen dining hall is a gathering place for the big family. As the children grow up, the small suite can be turned into home for married couple, and the two generations can still have their own space. When the young couple have their own children and move out, the small suite can be Airbnb, or lease to urban white-collar workers, and the open kitchen can be turned into a coffeeshop. So the old couple can have new partners and extra income for their retirement life. The addition of this small garden of 10sqm not only enriches the relationships between public and private spaces of the house, but also brings more possibilities.

邻里关系图
Neighborhood Relations Diagram

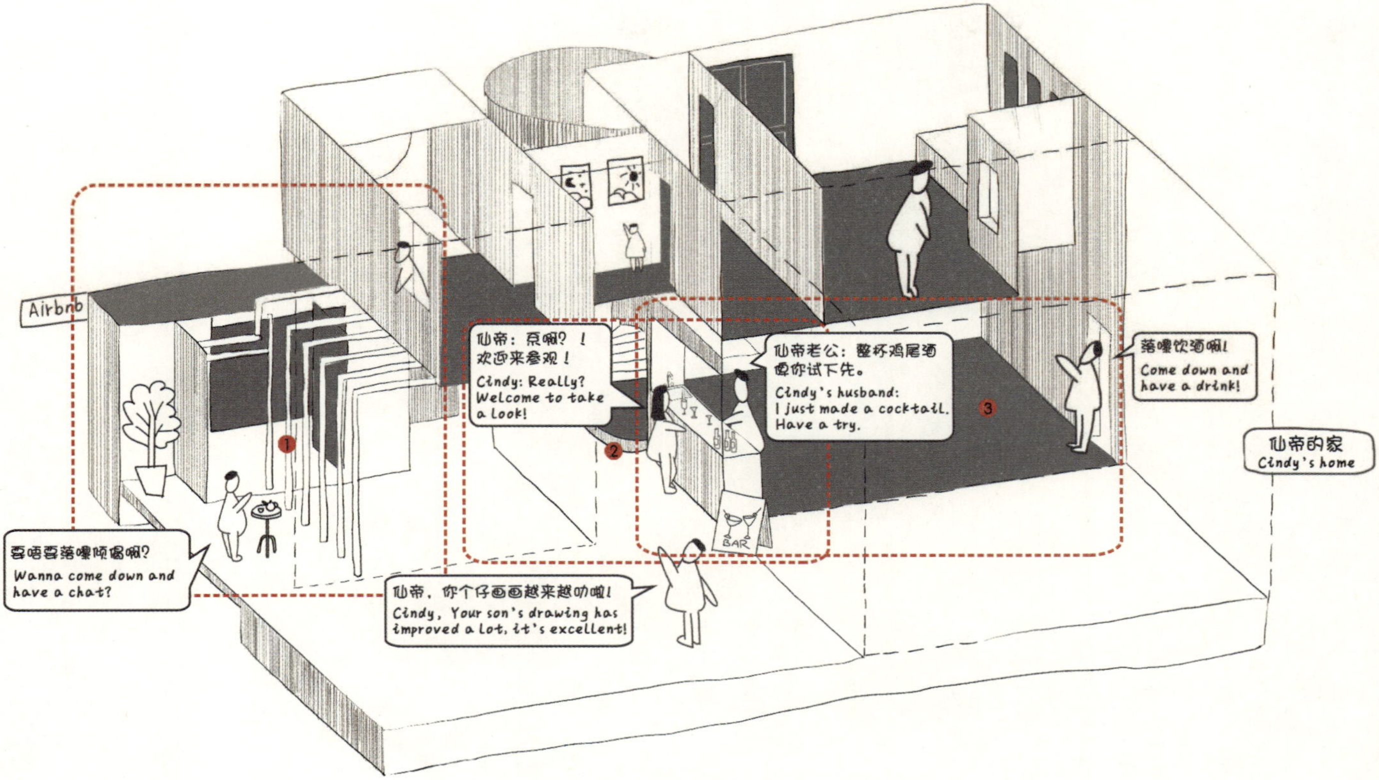

① 大套房与小套房共用的门前花园
The front garden shared by the big and small flats

② 是边界也是共用厨房
It's both a border and a shared kitchen

③ 书房与 Airbnb 的上下对望空间
The study upstairs and the Airbnb small flat downstairs

双面使用的厨房,模糊房屋内外边界
Double-sided kitchen blurring interior and exterior boundaries of the house

两代人的共享厨房
The kitchen shared by two generations

Airbnb 接待区
Airbnb reception area

二手书店
The second-hand bookshop

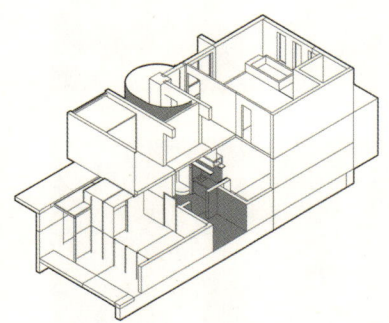

花园厨房在仙帝家的空间位置图
Garden kitchen's location in Cindy's home

①

②

③

④

⑤

⑥

⑦

⑧

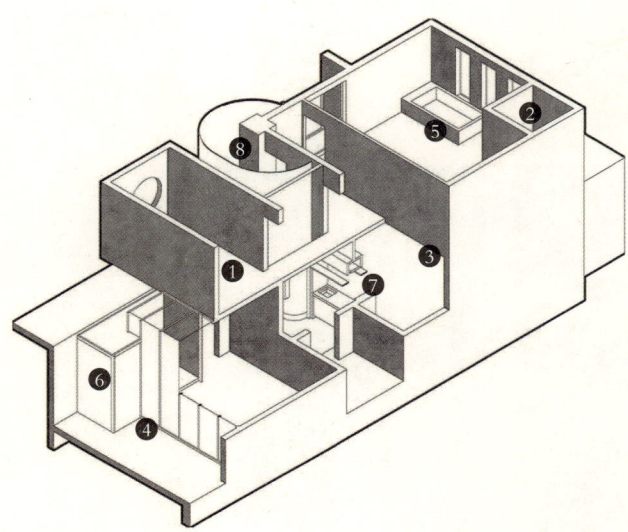

仙帝的家空间构成
Space composition of Cindy's home

① 为仙帝书房创作的艺术品"金帘"
  The artwork "Golden Curtain" created for Cindy's study

② 联通卧室与客厅的内天井
  The inner patio connecting the bedroom and the living room

③ 利用旧墙面创作的"黄金雨"装置
  An installation named "Golden Rain" created by making use of the old wall

④⑥ 可以在花树下沐浴夕阳的彩色浴室
  The colorful bathroom for bathing in the light of a setting sun under blossoms

⑤ 二楼卧室一角
  A corner of the bedroom the second floor

⑦ 夜晚的双边厨房
  The bilateral kitchen at night

⑧ PVC水管制成的楼梯立面
  The staircase facade made of PVC water pipes

创建邻里关系的立面
The facade that creates neighborhood relationship

书房里的茶空间也可兼作卧室,一个圆窗把普普通通的南方农村勾勒得如诗如画
The tea space in the study can also be used as bedroom, and the ordinary southern countryside viewed from the round window looks so picturesque and poetic

骑楼竹筒屋
Qilou Long House

老本的家： 250 平方米有骑楼和天井的房子
Old Ben's home: A 250sqm house with Qilou and patio

职业：天使投资人
Occupation: Angel investor

斜杠爱好：艺术收藏、摄影、美食
Hobbies: Art collection, photography, gourmet

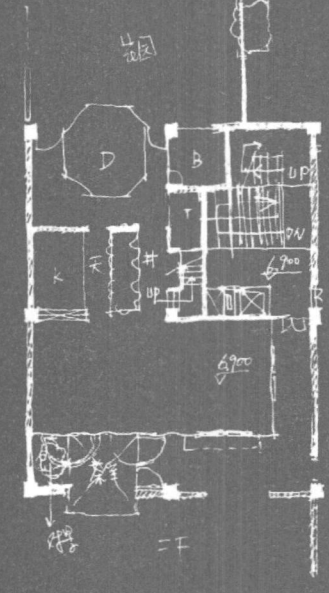

这是最接近我童年回忆的一个户型：门口是宽阔高大的骑楼。以前骑楼是商住功能混合的建筑，既是遮风挡雨的商业步行街，也是家人吃饭、小孩跳格子、邻居打牌的地方。现在是半公共空间，邻居可以随时进入。面向骑楼的大厅更像一个展厅或者工作室。当时园区里有好几个茶室，也不常开，某次遇到老板在，"蹭"到上好茶，才知道他是做空调设备的生意，而非卖茶，只是把谈生意的"会议室"挪到茶室，偶尔还能遇上知己，品茶说道，不亦乐乎。工作室不是艺术家、设计师专属的，谁都可以把自己的爱好同别人分享，顺便在同好中找到合作伙伴。穿过这个既像茶室又像展厅的工作室是一个天井。儿时的回忆是昏暗潮湿的，搭建了各家各户透风漏雨的厨房、卫生间。于是我在天井做了个有芭蕉的半开放卫生间，想取个好听的名字"琐琐楼"，就是联想雨打芭蕉时"大珠小珠落玉盘"的声音。后以"琐碎"为题作了对联于门前。前店后居，有骑楼有天井，还原了广州传统民宅的建筑特色。

This house plan is the closest to my childhood memory: at the door there is a wide and tall Qilou, which in the old time was a building with mixed commercial and residential functions, not only sheltering the commercial pedestrian street from wind and rain, but also as a place for family meals, kids to "jump grids" and playing cards with neighbors. Now it is a semi-public space, and neighbors can enter at any time. The lobby facing the Qilou is more like an exhibition hall or studio. There used to be several teahouses in the park, which were closed most of the time. One day I met the boss and not only got the chance to taste super good tea, but also found out that his real business was selling air conditioning equipment instead of tea. He just moved the conference room for business negotiation to the teahouse, where he would occasionally encounter like-minded friends to have a good chat over tea—what a pleasant thing! The studio is not exclusive to artists and designers; anyone can come to share their hobbies with others and may find suitable partners by the way. Passing through this tearoom or exhibition-hall like studio, there is a patio. In my childhood memory, the kitchens and bathrooms of each household were dark and damp with leakages for wind and rain to get in. So I build a semi-open bathroom with plantains in the patio and want a pleasant-sounding name for it such as "Suo Suo", which reminds me of the sound of raindrops hitting the plantain leaves like big and small beads falling on a jade plate. Later, I made a couplet themed on "Suo Sui (literally meaning triviality)" on the doorjamb. With shop in the front and home in the back, as well as Qilou and patio, now the two major architectural features of Guangzhou's traditional commercial residential building are restored.

邻里关系图
Neighborhood Relations Diagram

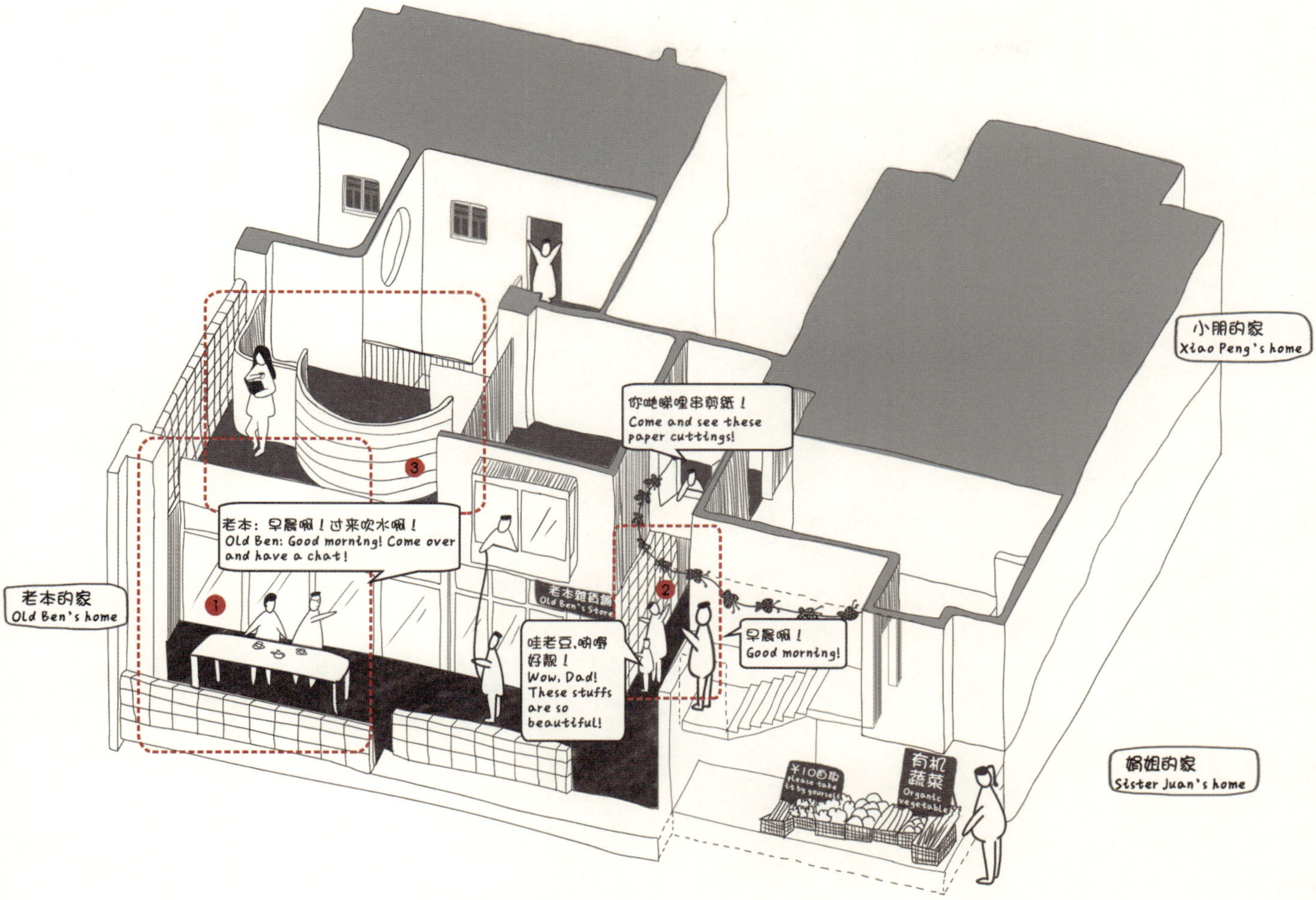

① 两层通高的骑楼玄关
Two-storey Qilou porch

② 一边是沙龙/客厅，一边是朝向楼内巷道的展览空间
On one side is the salon/living room and on the other side is an exhibition space facing the street

③ 面向骑楼街的卧室
The bedroom facing the Qilou street

楼房里的巷道空间
Alleyway space in the building

展览橱窗
Exhibition window

社区图书馆
Community library

攀岩空间
Rock climbing space

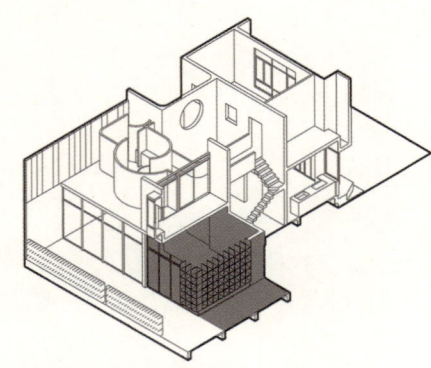

展示空间在老本家的空间位置
Exhibition space's location in Old Ben's home

①

②

③

④

⑤
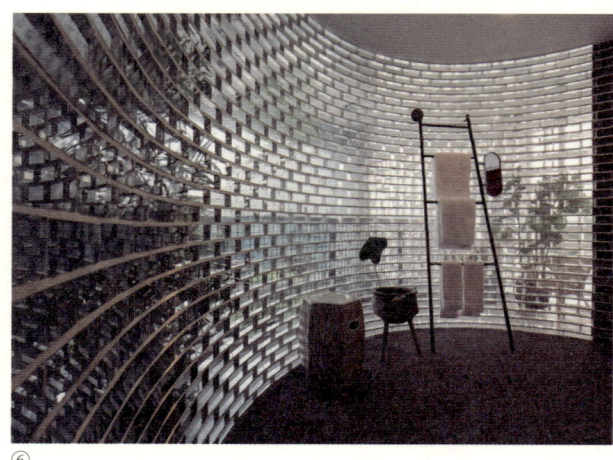
⑥

⑦

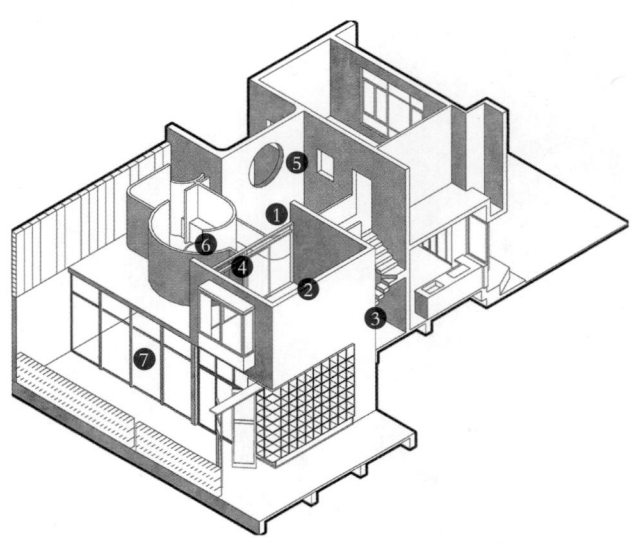

老本的家空间构成
Space composition of Old Ben's home

① 可以听到雨打芭蕉的洗手间
A toilet where one can hear raindrops pattering on plantain leaves

② 以瓦楞纸作为建筑平面装饰卧室回应工厂的前半生
Using corrugated paper to make architectural plane as a horizontal decoration to reflect the first half of the factory's life

③ 自制楼梯灯
Originally made staircase lamp

④ 提取自房间平面图元素的自创灯具
Originally created lamps with elements extracted from the room plan

⑤ 同属卧室的内窗与外窗
Inner and outer windows of the same bedroom

⑥ 半透明的弧形玻璃砖墙模糊花园与浴室
Semitransparent curved glass brick wall blurring garden and bathroom

⑦ 面向街道的展示性会客厅
Exhibition hall / living room facing the street

两层通高的骑楼式玄关
Two-storey Qilou like porch

走廊上的过街楼
Cross-street building on the corridor

给孩子造个大玩具
Building a Big Toy for Children

小 C 的家：200 平方米有坡的房子
Little C's home: A 200sqm house with ramp

职业：皮具设计师
Occupation: Leather designer

斜杠爱好：带孩子做甜品、面包作为教育方式
Hobbies: Making dessert and bread with children as a way of education

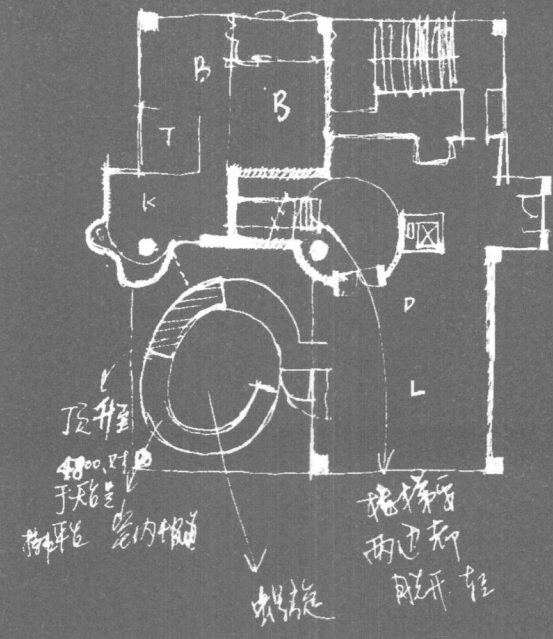

我很喜欢设计楼梯，常常赋予其超越交通功能的含义，例如设计一个富有体验感的楼梯鼓励日常使用，从而减少电梯的运作。对于一套两层 200 平方米的小复式，这个占据 1/4 面积的上下交通通道显得有点奢侈。但每次看到来访的小朋友流连忘返，便觉我们的初衷没有偏差。灵感源于一次去一个朋友家跟她讨论房子的设计，她租住的别墅，客厅就是工作室，楼梯包着厚厚的毯子以防孩子撞伤，我想：要是把楼梯改成滑道，孩子和宠物狗都会很开心吧！当然我们也不会只为孩子。当一个人很安静地穿越这个坡道的时候，仿如走入桃花源——经过一段渐暗空间，前方"仿佛若有光"，继续前行便是"柳暗花明又一村"。后来发现，使用者更有创意，居然有人把这里当作展厅使用，把坡道变成黑色 mini 版的古根海姆博物馆。有趣的设计会让人变得更有趣。

I love to design staircase and often give it a meaning beyond its traffic function; for example, to design a staircase providing interesting experience, so that people would rather walk the stairs than using elevator. For a two-storey small duplex of merely 200sqm, this traffic facility occupying 1/4 of the area seems a bit extravagant. But every time we see the visiting kids happily lingering here, we feel that our original intention is not deviated. I got the inspiration from a visit to a friend's home to discuss house design. In the villa she rented, the living room is also studio and the stairs are wrapped in thick blankets to prevent kids from bumping against it. Therefore, I think, if the staircase is turned into a ramp, kids and dogs must be very happy! Of course, it is not just for the kids; when one quietly passes through the ramp, he/she would feel like walking toward the "Peach Blossom Land"—at the end of the dark space, there is light dimly seen, and just move forward through the "dark willows and bright flowers", there is another village ahead. Of course, the users are more creative, and some people actually use it as an exhibition hall, turning the ramp into a black mini version of Guggenheim Museum. Interesting design also makes people more interesting.

邻里关系图
Neighborhood Relations Diagram

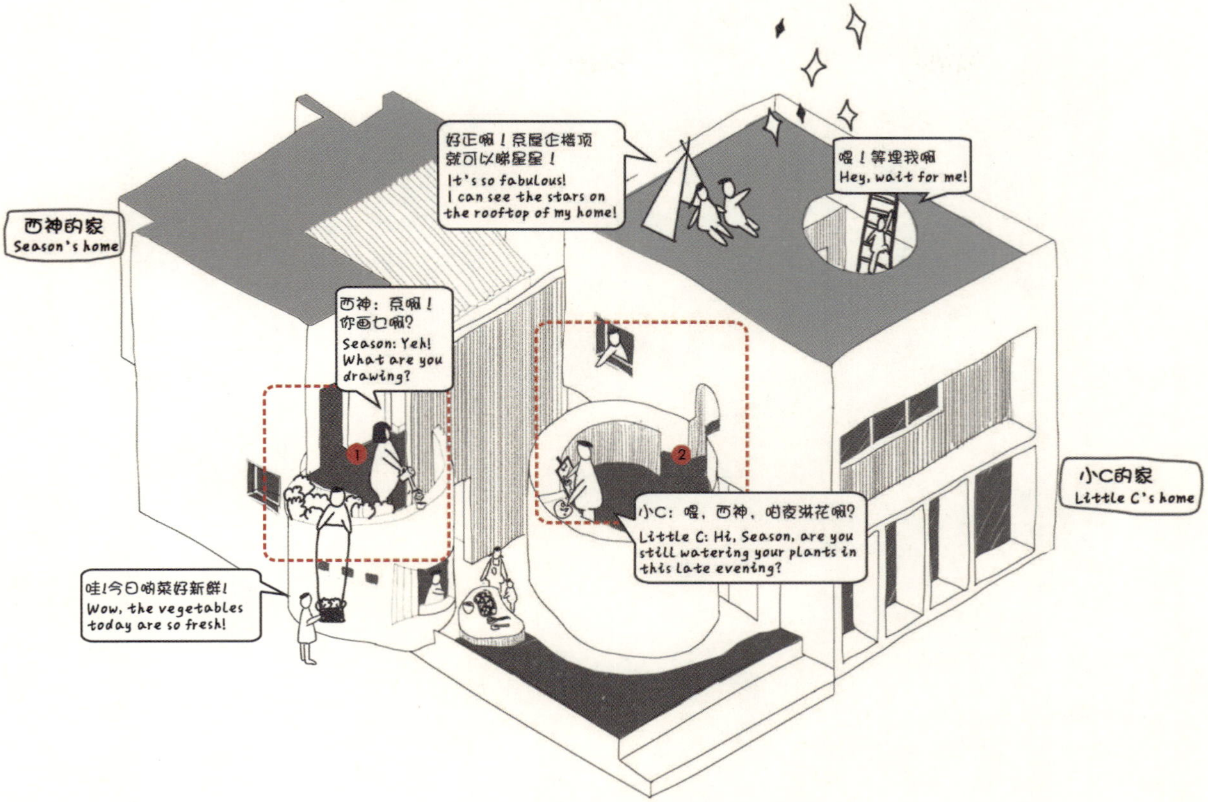

① 远看弧形坡道与西神家的露台
A distant view of the curved ramp and balcony of Season's home

② 从房间看室外敞厅
A view of the outdoor open hall from the room

缓坡联系上下层,大人和小孩都能找到各自的乐趣
The gentle ramp connects the two floors, so both kids and adults can enjoy themselves in their own ways

儿童乐园
Children's playground

人宠空间
Space for people and pets

展览
Exhibition

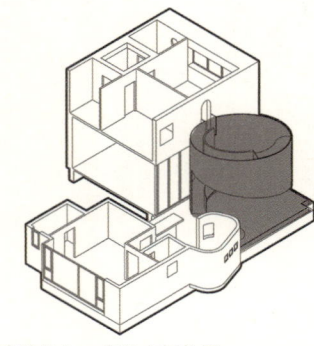

坡道在小 C 家的空间位置
The ramp's location in Little C's home

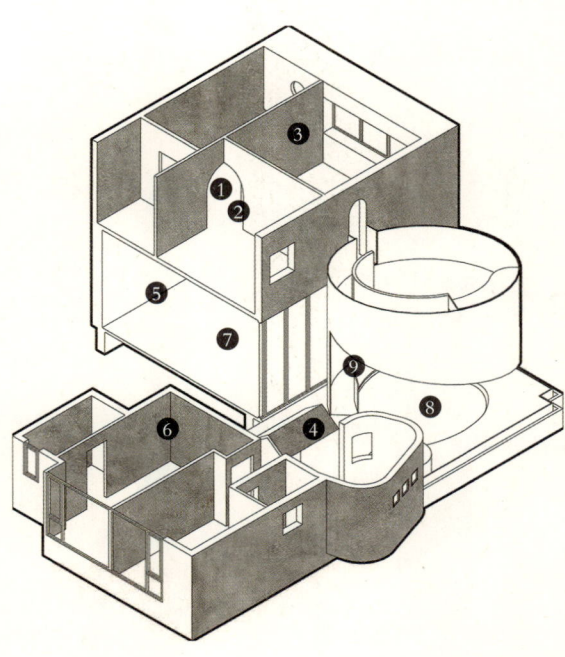

小 C 的家空间构成
Space composition of Little C's home

①② 无界——卧室、休息区与卫生间由三拱门彼此区分又相互连通
　　Borderless—the bedroom, living room and lounge are both separated and connected with each other by three arches

③ 呼应三拱门空间创作的灯光装置
　　The tailor-made lighting device echoes the three-arch space

④ 施工结束后，为处理消防喇叭创作的灯具
　　Upon completion of the construction, a lighting device was custom-made to conceal the fire horn

⑤ 以不做装修的土建材料——红砖墙，模糊室内外
　　Red-brick wall, a non-decorative raw material is adopted to blur the boundary between indoor and outdoor spaces

⑥ 次卧室一角
　　A corner of the secondary bedroom

⑦ 从客厅/工作室看坡道花园
　　A view of the garden with ramp from the living room/studio

⑧ 傍晚从坡道俯视花园
　　A downward view of the garden from the ramp in the evening

⑨ 坡道正投影下的水池也是花园的安全边界
　　The pool directly below the ramp is also the safety boundary of the garden

客厅也是工作室
The living room can also be a studio

握手楼
Shaking-hand building

六个好友的家
The Home of Six Friends

房子是这样盖起来的……
This is how the house is built…

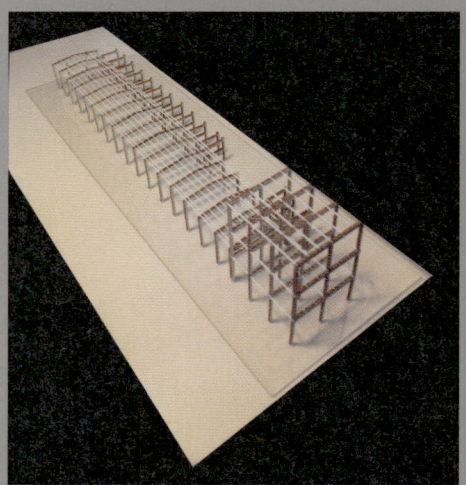

建筑原有的"多米诺"框架
The original "Domino" framework of the building

模块式的组合
Modular Combination

小C的家：
200平方米有坡的房子
Little C's home:
A 200sqm house with ramp

仙蒂的家：
230平方米有桥的房子
Cindy's home:
A 230sqm house with bridge
详见 62 页
See Page 62 for details

小鹏的家：
80平方米有天井的房子
Xiao Peng's home:
An 80sqm house with pavilion
详见 78 页
See Page 78 for details

娟姐的家：
80平方米有廊的房子
Sister Juan's home:
An 80sqm house with veranda
详见 42 页
See Page 42 for details

四神的家：
35平方米有天池的房子
Season's home:
A 35sqm house with "heaven lake"

加厚的立面
Thickened Facade

由个体的使用需求生成立面。

这个三层的机电塔楼就是山，身边几个"斜杠青年"来占山开田。他们都是梦想家，希望自己的工作室前庭后院，可以躺在浴池看星星，可以工作，又可以安居会友，还希望自己不用的时候可以做 Airbnb……最重要的，是猫犬相闻常相往来。

南、北两个消防楼梯连成"山路"。沿路搭建了形态各异、高低不同的 6 套房子，在这个 15 米 × 18 米 × 13.2 米的厂房空间内，装进了一个立体的村落，一个垂直的园林。

这是个没有围墙的园林。除了保留部分尚稳固的洗石米外墙，其余开放并外挑 600 毫米形成"加厚边界"。这里有花园里的书房、看得到星星的浴室、充满阳光的菜园。按各住户的需求划分空间，各据一方。

项目先通过"减法"挖出各家必要的阳台空间，再用"加法"搭建各户需要的浴室、温室、楼梯。建筑加固的构件形成"博古架"式的立面特征。当花木成长起来，人的生活进入其间，厂房就被营造成一个巨大的太湖石，孔洞内滋养着活色生香的生活日常。

在多米诺框架实现个体的多样性需求
To meet diversified needs of individuals in the "Domino" framework

建筑原状表皮
Original skin of the building

按照每户需求"挖出"阳台
"Digging out" balconies based on needs of each household

部分功能组件外挑 600 毫米，增加立面的厚度
Some functional components extend 600mm outward to increase the thickness of the facade

调整开窗位置，增加纵横向遮阳板
Adjusting window position to increase sunshade on both longitudinal and transverse directions

植物开始生长，生活围绕花园展开
When plants begin to grow, people's lives tend to unfold

The facade is generated by the needs of individual users.

The three-storey tower is like a hill for my "slash youth" friends to claim and plow their plots. They are all dreamers, hoping to have their own studios, with front and back yards, lying in the bathtub while watching stars, working and socializing with friends, and putting the house on Airbnb when they are not using it. And most importantly, they could hear the pets next door and drop around regularly.

The south and north fire escape stairs are connected to form a hill path. Six houses with different shapes and heights are built along the path, while a three-dimensional village and a vertical garden are installed in the factory space of 15m×18m×13.2m.

It is a garden without walls. In addition to retaining some of the still stable cement exterior walls, the rest are open and overhang by 600mm to form a "thickened border", which accommodates a study room in the garden, a bathroom with starlight, and a vegetable garden full of sunshine. By coordinating the needs of each household to divide the space, everyone can have his own dream house.

"Subtraction" is applied to "dig out" the essential balcony for each household and then "addition" is adopted to build bathroom, greenhouse and staircase according to particular needs of the residents. The building's structure is reinforced to form a facade looking like "antique-and-curio cabinet". With trees and flowers growing and blooming, and people living among them, the factory building is turned into a huge holey Taihu stone, which accommodates and nourishes the daily life shimmering with all colors and fragrances.

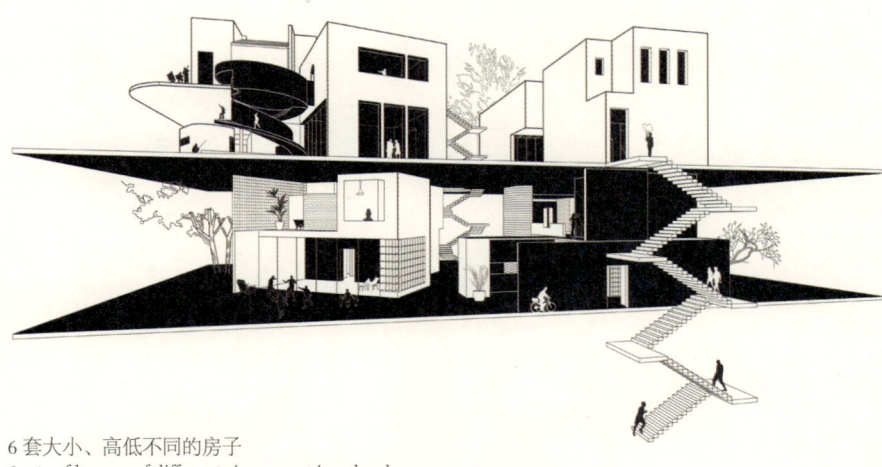

6 套大小、高低不同的房子
6 sets of houses of different sizes on various levels

柯林·罗在《透明性》中这样描述:"包豪斯校舍利用大量透明材质的立面元素,创造了建筑整体的通透感。而勒·柯布西耶设计的加歇别墅则反其道而行之,并没有采用过多的透明材质,而是利用空间的交叠与渗透,创造了建筑空间的透明感。"① 可以说,勒·柯布西耶没有去"设计"这个外立面,而是通过设计平面,以空间直接构成(或者生成)了外立面。在紫泥十二门无界社区这个项目中,我们同样不去"设计"立面,而是由6套房子的前庭后院和"僭建物"共同构成(生成)了外立面。这好比拆除了围墙的园子,亭台楼阁前后叠置,显出"漏透"的山、石品相。董豫赣在《石山壹品》中写道,"郭熙的山水,常以亭台楼阁,标识山中居游胜所;李公麟的这幅山水,却拟大量的山洞与山台,因类似于厅堂与庭院,则成为最经典的山居组合……"。② 我们正尝试用柯林·罗描述的透明性转译为李公麟《龙眠山庄图》中的居游胜景——从山外窥见家家户户隐约的庭院厅堂,忍不住要去一探究竟。碎片化的立面自然无须以极简主义之名去统一材料和色彩。紫泥堂创意园区自20世纪50年代至90年代一直在建设发展,好比一个建材博物馆。我们从中摘取时间的片段,运用了多达13种物料去搭建6个小屋,仿如自建房屋的自由状态。由大大小小的搭建空间构成的立面展现了各家各户活色生香的生活画面,是古代山水画的现代拼贴版。

我们在试图模糊室内外的边界,把自然或抽象或具体地纳入建筑内。以"加厚边界"的方式把空间存在所依附的表皮转换为空间本身,模糊了两者的定义。

In his book *Transparency* ①, Colin Rowe mentioned that the Bauhaus dormitory realized the transparency of the whole building via extensive use of transparent elevational elements; while by contrast, in Le Corhusier's villa at Garches, a transparency of the architectural space is effected not through the agency of a mass of transparent materials but rather through the overlapping and interpenetration of space. We may say that Le Corhusier didn't "design" the facade, but through graphic design, the facade is constructed (or generated) by space directly. Similarly, in the Zi Ni Twelve Portals project, we didn't "design" the facade but let it be generated by the courtyards and backyards of the 6 houses jointly with the "unauthorized building works". It could be compared to a garden whose fences have been removed, thus mountain and rocks could be seen through the pavilions, terraces and towers that

---

① [美]柯林·罗,罗伯特·斯拉茨基. 透明性[M]. 金秋野,王又佳译. 北京:中国建筑工业出版社,2008.
Colin Rowe, Robert Slutzky. Transparency[M]. Jin Qiuye, Wang Youjia, translator. Beijing: China Architecture & Building Press, 2008.
② 王欣,金秋野. 乌有园 第2辑 幻梦与真实[M]. 上海:同济大学出版社,2017.
Wang Xin, Jin Qiuye. Arcadia Volume II Illusion & Reality[M]. Shanghai: Tongji University Press, 2017.

《龙眠山庄图》(局部)
The Mountain Villa of Sleeping Dragon (partial)

加歇别墅·透明性
Villa Gachet · Transparency

are placed in a way "without optical destruction of each other". Dong Yugan wrote in his essay *Appreciating Rockwork as Mountain* that, "In Guo Xi's mountain and water works, the scenic spots and resorts in mountains are often named after pavilions, terraces and towers; while in this painting by Li Gonglin, there are lots of caves and maintain terraces that become classical combination for maintain dwelling thanks to their remarkable resemblance to pavilions, terraces and towers."② We are attempting to translate the transparency described by Colin into the scenic journey in Li Gonglin's *The Mountain Villa of Sleeping Dragon*—a peep into the courtyards and sitting rooms of the mountain villas would lure one to explore further. The fragmented facade surely doesn't need to be unified in terms of material and color in the name of minimalism. The Zi Ni Tang Park was undergoing constant construction and development from 1950s to 1990s and has thus become a museum of building materials. We just picked one piece from its history and used 13 kinds of material to build 6 houses in order to simulate the free state of a privately built property. The unique facade, which consists of constructed spaces of various sizes, provides shortcuts for the neighbors and their pets to drop around, so the people here would be as happy as their counterparts lingering around in pavilions and caves among mountains in ancient paintings.

We attempt to blur the boundaries between the interior and the exterior, and to bring nature into architecture in both abstract and concrete ways. Adopting an approach of "broadening the border" to turn the surface, on which the space depends, into the space, the definitions of both interior and exterior become ambiguous.

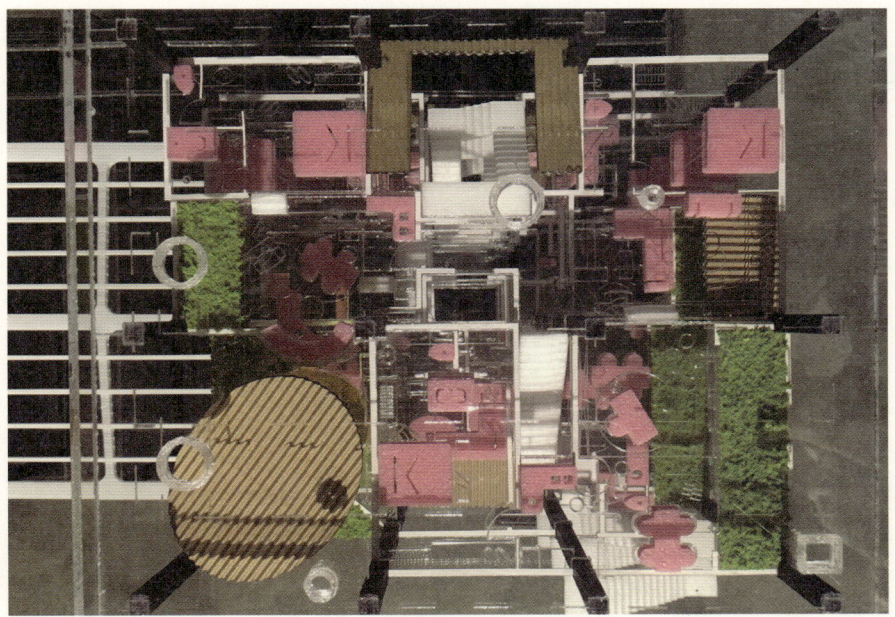

在原有的柱网框架中根据不同用户的需求分配房间和花园的占比
In the original framework of the column network, the area of room and garden is allocated according to the needs of different users

东立面效果图（绘制于 2017 年 1 月）
East elevation rendering (drawn in January, 2017)

场景一：共享客厅
Scene 1: Shared living room

场景二：家就是美术馆
Scene 2: Home is art museum

场景三：生活剧场
Scene 3: Life theater

自由的平面
Free Planes

"用户自定义功能"：每套房子都有"自建空间"让住户发挥创意。例如一个花园里的浴池，住家可以用来种植，做展览的时候就是水上展厅，做工作室的时候就是"头脑风暴空间"。

展览 / 画廊 / 商店
EXHIBITION / GALLERY / SHOP

办公区 / 工作坊
OFFICE / WORKSHOP

起居室
HOUSE

二层平面图情景一
Senario 1 of 2nd floor plan

二层平面图情景二
Senario 2 of 2nd floor plan

三层平面图情景一
Senario 1 of 3rd floor plan

三层平面图情景二
Senario 2 of 3rd floor plan

"User-defined Function": Each house has "self-built space" for residents to play a creative role. For example, a bath in the garden can be used for planting on usual days, and serve as "exhibition hall on water" or even "brainstorming room" for studio when needed.

四层平面图情景一
Senario 1 of 4th floor plan

四层平面图情景二
Senario 2 of 4th floor plan

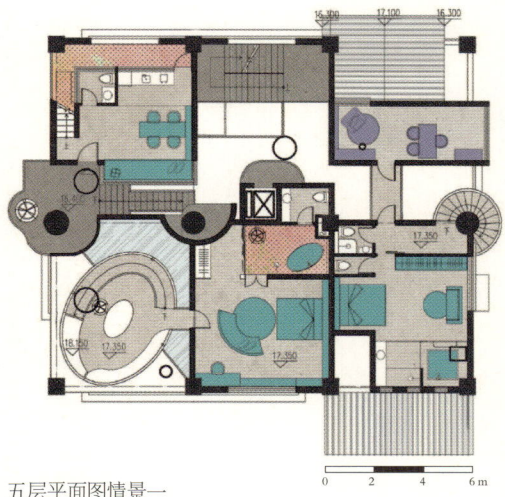

五层平面图情景一
Senario 1 of 5th floor plan

五层平面图情景二
Senario 2 of 5th floor plan

六个好友的家
The Home of Six Friends

在无界社区里,每一个角落都可以是我们共同的客厅……
In the Borderless Community, every corner is our shared living room...

天台
Rooftop

①

②

③

④

⑤

①② 天台的日与夜
Day and night of the roof

③ 屋顶花园的围栏以弧线呼应，天台是鸟瞰全厂观赏大烟囱的最佳位置
The fence of the rooftop garden echoes the environment with wavy shape and the rooftop is the best place to have a bird's eye view of the chimney

④⑤ 四周山峦起伏，组合出不同尺度的围合空间，可以约三五知己小酌放歌……这是大家的空中客厅，放电影、赏月区、舞蹈课室……，亦可以聚会
Surrounded by hills, spaces of different scales can be enclosed to serve different functions such as drinking and singing with several friends, watching movie, appreciating the moon, having dance classes or throwing a big party. This is a living room in the air for everyone

⑥ 天台平面图
Roof plan

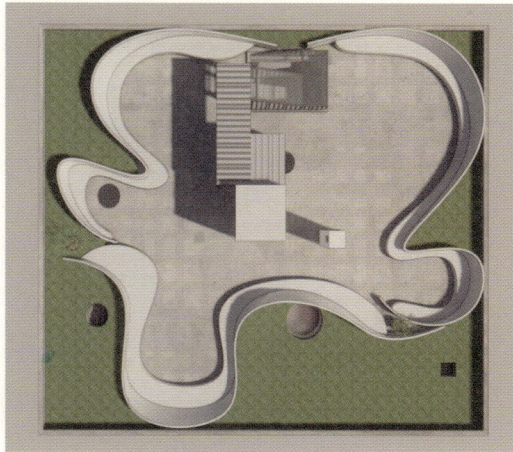
⑥

97

围墙
Walls

旧围墙（2015 年）
Old wall (2015)

改造前（2018 年 3 月）
Before transformation (March, 2018)

改造前平面图
Plan before transformation

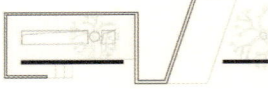

改造后平面图
Plan after transformation

艺术营造 © 扉
Artecture© FEI

房子盖好了，缺个"前奏"。恰好楼前有一幅旧墙，不如再次用加厚的方法，把实变空，等待着被重新定义。作为边界的墙，被加厚扩展成多个露天展厅，被人的活动"侵蚀"，成为无界社区的门户，是对"无界"最好的诠释。

When the house is completed, it needs a "prelude". It happens that there is an old wall in front of the building, so we decided to use the "thickening" method again to empty the solid and turn it into a space to be redefined. While being boundary, the wall is "invaded" by human activities and is expanded into several open-air exhibition halls, serving as gateway to the Borderless Community. This is the best interpretation of "borderless".

茶室
Teahouse

三五朋友聚会的空间
Space for small gatherings

婚纱照片场
Venue for taking wedding photos

花档 / 墟
Flower stall/Bazaar

工作坊场地
Venue for workshops

舞台 / 小剧场
Stage/Mini theater

新围墙把旧围墙当作展品"装裱"起来
The old wall is "mounted" by the new one like an exhibit

对应园区遗留的"小心来车"画了一满幅的眼睛,成为打卡秘境
Corresponding to the "Be careful of coming cars" warning left over from the park, a picture full of eyes was painted on the wall, which has become a secret "Instagram Hotspot"

电影院 / 瑜伽房 / 展厅……
Cinema/Yoga Room/Exhibition Hall...

多功能厅内梯田式台阶
Terraced steps in the multi-functional hall

多功能厅的聚碳酸酯板外墙
The polycarbonate exterior wall of the multi-functional hall

瑜伽课
Yoga class

年会活动
Annual staff party

影院
Cinema

未来，如何共同生活
How to Live Together in the Future

与大众一起设计
Design with the public

建筑师的思考

长江/三江汇流

- 个体存在遗存的可识别性

现代主义·图案派

- 现代化主义X——不仅仅建造方法设计
- 符合体系的多个体符合法则的组合
- 形成的抽象

作为一门社会学科的建筑学

- 自我与共建
- 社区意象
- 美与关怀

山水园林·诗意栖居

大部分之后演变后到现代：春·冬·雨·雾·雪·阴·林·巷·院
《园林的感知事象》 引《浮生六记》为同时期作品

基本列表：250年万米 有酒精和太阳的院子

楼梯间室：80平方米 有画的院子

小院室：80平方米 冷冬季节的院子

·书店	街道	
·餐厅		
·展示间		
·儿童活动站	多向维交通空间	
·展示间		
·开阔	探访丰富花园	
·封闭		
·明亮		
·阴暗		
·夜晚	日常生活的展示	
·黄昏		
·运行		

楼梯通水流层	
交流空间	
书房室·储物室	
走廊上·卫生间	
有风光的院子	房
很其意的街道	楼
传感社会的观念	

80万平方米的地块尺度本身已经带来了，同了两个也被栅栏隔断：若提到南北"南方"。
成为了城市的基本组织元素：邻里街坊等，街区空间、社区活动...

为启蒙者和活跃的新市民化创造出日：在这我建议代代活者上重入之那万年方·
得无规整本整齐可言。其实只有2-3万米的场地和一般的可以纪念

似乎还比较大桥，工作着居个人来城的路径：构造出就是生活体方式一颜底…
接收高大方式组成"社交"

2019 年 1 月，"一条"采访扉建筑设计的紫泥十二门无界社区。6 个好友改造一个工厂车间，一起办展、一起开读书会、一起遛娃的乌托邦生活引发热议，翌日便登上热搜头条。Co-living 成为大众共同的向往。

2019 年 7 月，2020 威尼斯建筑双年展公布策展主题"我们将如何共同生活？"。无界社区似乎就是这样一个"我们可以从容'共同生活'的地方"："共同"是在个人独立性见长以外，对数字化和实体空间中的相互联系的渴望；"共同"是为新的家庭寻找更加多元化而有尊严的居住环境；"共同"是社区对公平、包容和空间认同需求的整合。

然而普遍的现实是，千篇一律的房产开发如何容纳个性化的创造？个体的空间生产实践如何把房子变成家？我们开始思考如何把无界社区改进推广以满足"人民日益增长的美好生活需要"。

In January 2019, "Yitiao" covered the Borderless Community of Zi Ni Twelve Portals designed by FEI Architects and posted a video clip about the "Utopian life" of 6 friends, who transformed a factory workshop into a co-living tower where they can hold exhibitions, read books and raise their kids together. It soon aroused heated discussion and became the hottest hashtag on Weibo the next day. Co-living has become the common aspiration of the general public.

In July 2019, theme for the Venice Biennale of Architecture 2020 was announced as "How will we live together?". The Borderless Community seems to be such a place where we can "live together" with ease and dignity: "together" is the desire for interconnectedness in both digital and physical spaces, in addition to our already acquired individual independence; "together" is to find a more diversified and dignified living environment for new families; "together" is the integration of community needs for equity, inclusiveness and spatial identity.

However, the general reality is that, how can the stereotyped property development accommodate the creation by individuals? How can the space production practiced by individuals turn a house into a home? We begin to think about how to improve and promote the Borderless Community to meet "the people's growing expectations for a better life".

资讯来源：新浪微博，数据截至 2021 年 1 月 15 日
Source: Sina Weibo, January 15, 2021

线下工作坊现场
The Site of Off-line Workshop

2020年1月,突如其来的新冠肺炎疫情使"隔离"成为关键词。我们的生活方式发生改变,家作为最后的堡垒,未来会是怎样?所有人都重新思考:"我们将如何共同生活?"

我们是否可以"共同"设计我们的"共同生活"?

2020年10月我们发起"未来的家"公众参与工作坊及系列学术研讨会,以线上及线下游戏"6个好友喊你来拼房"启动用户调研。项目包括4个周末的线下现场工作坊及为期一个月的线上工作坊,并和保利置业、一兜糖联合收集数据,共同研发"未来的家"概念屋设计。

100年前包豪斯提出"为大众设计"。今天,我们"与大众一起设计"。

In January 2020, the sudden outbreak of COVID-19 made "quarantine" as the keyword in people's life. Our way of life is bound to change. While home as the last fortress, what will our future be? It is time for everyone to reflect on the issue: "How will we live together?"

Can we design our "living together" together?

In October 2020, we launched the "Future Home" Public Participation Workshop and a series of academic seminars, as well as a user research with the on-line and off-line game "Six friends are calling you to share a house". The project includes four weekend off-line on-site workshops and a one-month on-line workshop, and data collection together with Poly Real Estate and Yidoutang in a joint effort to develop the conceptual design of "Future Home".

100 years ago, Bauhaus put forward the idea of "design for the public". Today, let's "design with the public".

线上游戏互动界面
The Interactive Interface of On-line Game

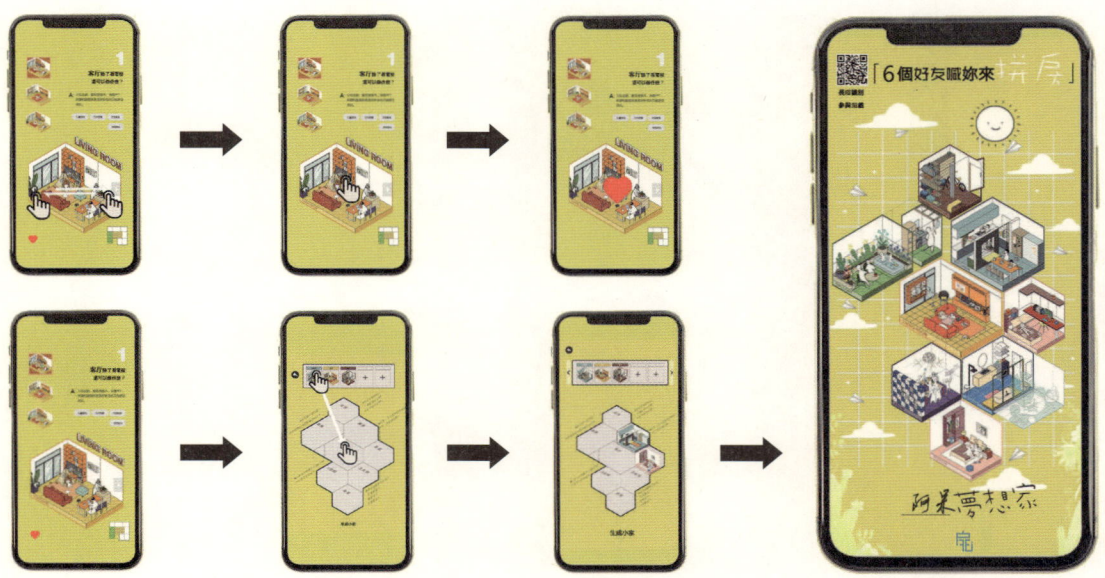

相机识别二维码，通过打开网页体验线上互动游戏
Use camera to scan the QR Code and open relevant web pages to experience on-line interactive games

线上工作坊群组讨论
Group Discussion of the On-line Workshop

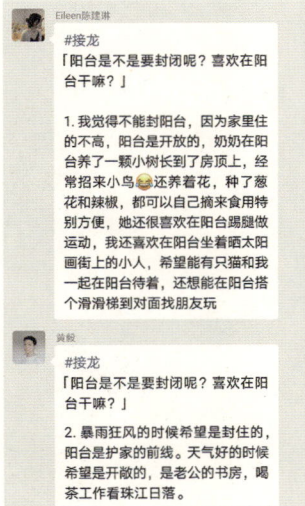
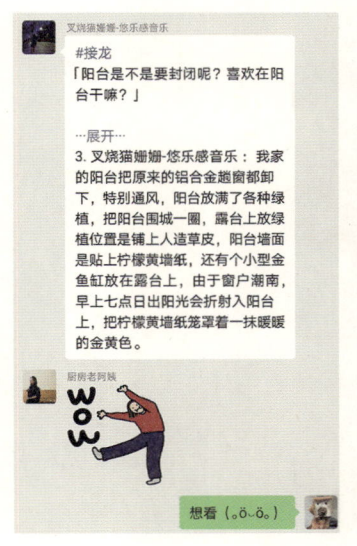
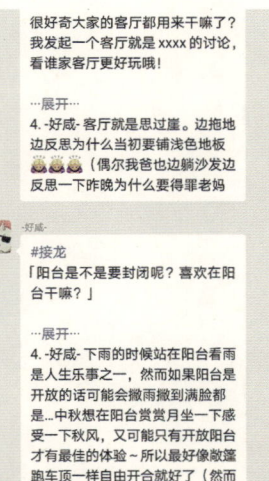

109

竹丝岗无界社区
Borderless Community of Zhusigang

建筑师自述
The Architect's Narration

何志森
Jason Zhisen Ho

华南理工大学建筑学院副研究员
扉合伙人、扉学术顾问、扉美术馆馆长
Mapping 工作坊创始人

Associate Research Fellow, School of Architecture, South China University of Technology
Partner, Academic Consultant of FEI, Curator of FEI Arts
Founder of Mapping Workshop

农林菜市场坐落于广州一个社群混杂和阶层分化较明显的老社区——东山口竹丝岗社区。2018至2020年期间，我在华南理工大学建筑学院发起了一个名为"菜市场美术馆"的菜市场改造课程。

自2018年起，我带领华南理工大学建筑学院的学生来到与扉美术馆一墙之隔的农林菜市场，观察和记录44位摊贩的真实生活和需求，挖掘他们背后不为人知的故事，在菜市场内外和他们一起完成一系列的创作，最终这些创作神奇地将不同阶层和文化背景的人群联结在了一起。和今天被资本与权力主导的社区改造模式不一样的是，这个项目完全没有触碰菜市场看似破旧不堪的物理空间，而是通过一系列极其柔软的介入甚至是不造物的方式来重新构建摊贩生而为人的尊严和自信，在此基础上唤醒大众日益消逝的集体意识和对公共空间的主导意识，并将之转化为今天中国城市更新和社区营造最重要的一股力量。

2020年10月，这个陪伴了竹丝岗社区39年的菜市场因违建及环境原因被当地部门下令拆除。2021年7月，农林菜市场在重庆悦来美术馆"重建"。

Nonglin Market is located in Zhusigang area, one of Guangzhou's most mixed and divided communities. Between 2018 and 2020, several public-engaged renewal workshops led by me, in cooperation with School of Architecture, South China University of Technology, took place in this market.

To understand the vendors' real life and demands, all the architectural students in these workshops were required to work with them side by side in the market. During these periods of time, the students with the vendors completed a series of design interventions inside the market and around the community together, magically reconnecting people from all ranks and with various cultural backgrounds. Unlike today's community transformation model dominated by capital and power, this project does not touch the seemingly dilapidated physical space of the market at all, but reconstructs the dignity and self-confidence of the vendors through a series of extremely soft interventions or even non-creative ways, on the basis of which, it awakens the public to the fading sense of collectiveness and ownership over community, and turn it into the most critical force behind the ongoing urban renewal and community empowerment across China today.

In October 2020, this 39-year-old Nonglin Market was demolished by the local government due to legal and environmental reasons. In July 2021, Nonglin Market was "rebuilt" at Yuelai Art Museum of Chongqing.

2022 年 9 月
September, 2022

菜市场里的美术馆
A Museum in the Market

很多专业者喜欢把社区美化工程称为"社会设计",安排几个社区居民和设计师一起工作叫"公众参与",让中产阶级在公共空间自娱自乐说成是修复"人与人的关联"。今天,这些以"社区营造"为名义的城市更新运动正在加速城市活力的消失。农林菜市场改造项目就是在这种背景下发起的,旨在重新定义"社区改造"在社会分化和排斥背景下所担当的角色,并对当前的改造模式提出质疑。

Many professionals tend to refer to community beautification project as "social design", the arrangement of some community residents and designers to work together as "public participation", and the self-entertainment of middle class in public space as "repairing interpersonal relationship". Today, these urban renewal movements in the name of "community building" are accelerating the disappearance of urban vitality. The Nonglin Market transformation project was launched under this circumstance to redefine the role of "community transformation" in the context of severe social division and exclusion as well as to reflect upon and question the current transformation model.

已有39年历史的农林菜市场位于广州东山口竹丝岗社区的正中心。竹丝岗社区拥有全广州最好的医院、学校和最昂贵的公寓大楼,这些公寓大楼大部分被当地居民所拥有。与此同时,竹丝岗社区也居住着大量的低收入外来租客,如菜市场摊贩、快递员、环卫工人和病患家属等。这些外来租客蜗居的破旧楼房,和周边现代化的高楼大厦形成一种鲜明的对比,这也让竹丝岗社区成为社群比较混杂和阶层分化比较严重的社区之一。外来租客与本地居民之间的隔阂与冲突近年来愈演愈烈。

Nonglin Market is located in the heart of Zhusigang Community with a history of 39 years. Zhusigang has Guangzhou's most expensive apartment towers owned by the locals, in the same time, it is also filled with old and shabby residential houses occupied by low-income migrant workers like market vendors, deliverymen, sanitation workers and relatives of patients, etc. For a long time, Zhusigang has become one of Guangzhou's most mixed and divided communities. The conflict between the migrant workers and the local residents is getting intensified in recent years.

农林菜市场刚好紧挨着一个当代艺术机构——扉美术馆。 在2017年12月之前,扉美术馆周边有一堵很高的水泥墙,把菜市场完全排斥在外。为了让菜市场和美术馆之间的边界成为一个"连接"的景观,2017年12月艺术家

最初的分界墙
2017 年 12 月之前,菜市场和美术馆之间的一堵水泥墙

The Original Dividing Wall
Prior to December 2017, there was a concrete wall separating the market from the museum

无界的墙
2017 年 12 月,艺术家宋冬将这堵水泥墙改造成"无界的墙",它由数千件被拆除的胡同房屋的门窗制成

Borderless Wall
In December 2017, the artist Song Dong turned the concrete wall into an artwork titled "Borderless Wall" made of thousands of door and window pieces from demolished Hutong houses

宋冬用数千扇被拆除的北京胡同房屋的门和窗户把坚硬的水泥墙改造成一件名为"无界的墙"的艺术装置。为了真正成为社区里的一座"无界"美术馆，扉美术馆发起了一系列社区居民可以参与的艺术活动。其中一项是"百家宴"活动，扉美术馆想邀请不同阶层和文化背景的人沿着"无界的墙"一起吃饭。然而，一墙之隔的菜市场摊贩拒绝了邀请，他们对这样的社交活动表现得毫无兴趣。

Nonglin Market sits right next to FEI Arts, a local contemporary art museum. Prior to December 2017, there was a concrete wall separating the market from the museum. In December 2017, in order to make the boundary disappear, the museum invited artist Song Dong to turn the concrete wall into an artwork titled "Borderless Wall" which is made of thousands of door and window pieces from demolished Hutong houses. To further create connections, the museum launched a series of public-engaged art activities for both the migrant workers and the local residents, such as "hundred-family banquet" inviting people from all ranks and with various cultural backgrounds in Zhusigang to dine together along the Borderless Wall. However, the next-door market vendors turned down the invitation, showing no interest in such social interactions.

社区共建活动
菜市场摊主、竹丝岗社区居民、街头工作者及艺术家等不同人群参加由扉美术馆举办的一年一度的"百家宴"

Community-Engaged Activities
People in Zhusigang community dined together in the annual "hundred-family banquet" held by FEI Arts

2018至2020年，我带领华南理工大学建筑学院的学生在农林菜市场及其周边连续开展了4个公众参与的社区改造工作坊。在完全不清楚需要改造什么之前，每一位工作坊的学生都被要求与摊贩在菜市场并肩工作至少2个星期。在3年的时间里，学生和摊贩一起在菜市场和竹丝岗社区完成了一系列的艺术介入和空间改造项目。其中，"手美术馆"和"民众花园"就是两个打破阶层边界、重建联结的社区改造项目，让竹丝岗社区成为一个真正意义上的"无界社区"。

From 2018 to 2020, I led the students of the School of Architecture of South China University of Technology to carry out 4 public-engaged renewal workshops in a row at Nonglin Market and its neighborhood. Before knowing what needed to be renewed, all the students were required to work with the vendors side by side in the market for at least two weeks. During the three years, the students and the vendors together completed a series of artistic and design interventions in the market and around the Zhusigang community. Among them, "Hand Museum" and "People's Garden" were two projects that helped rebuild the interpersonal connections among people from different classes and truly made the Zhusigang community a "Borderless Community".

在"手美术馆"项目里，我们采取了一种轻微的、不造物的改造方式来修复菜市场摊贩和当地居民之间分裂的社会关系。在2018年第一次工作坊期间，学生们观察到顾客（主要是当地居民）与摊贩之间在过去的30多年基本没有太多的交流和互动，只有买卖上的关系。几乎所有的摊贩都把自己看成是这个社会最底层、最卑微的人。但在和摊贩一起工作的时候，学生们发现许多摊贩会自然而然地通过聊他们的双手以及分享双手背后的故事来展现他们的尊严和自信。对于摊贩来说，双手是他们所有幸福的来源，是他们最骄傲的"资本"。于是，我开始让学生为菜市场里所有的摊贩拍摄双手。

In the project of "Hand Museum", we employed a light and nonphysical way to restore the broken connections between the market vendors and the local residents. While working with the vendors during the first workshop in 2018, the students observed that in the past 30 years, there had been little communication and interaction between customers (mainly local residents) and vendors, and they only have interests in buying and selling. Almost all vendors regard themselves as the lowest and humblest group of people in society. However, the students found out that all the vendors were very happy to talk about their hands and share the stories behind their hands to show their dignity and self-confidence. For the vendors, their hands are the source

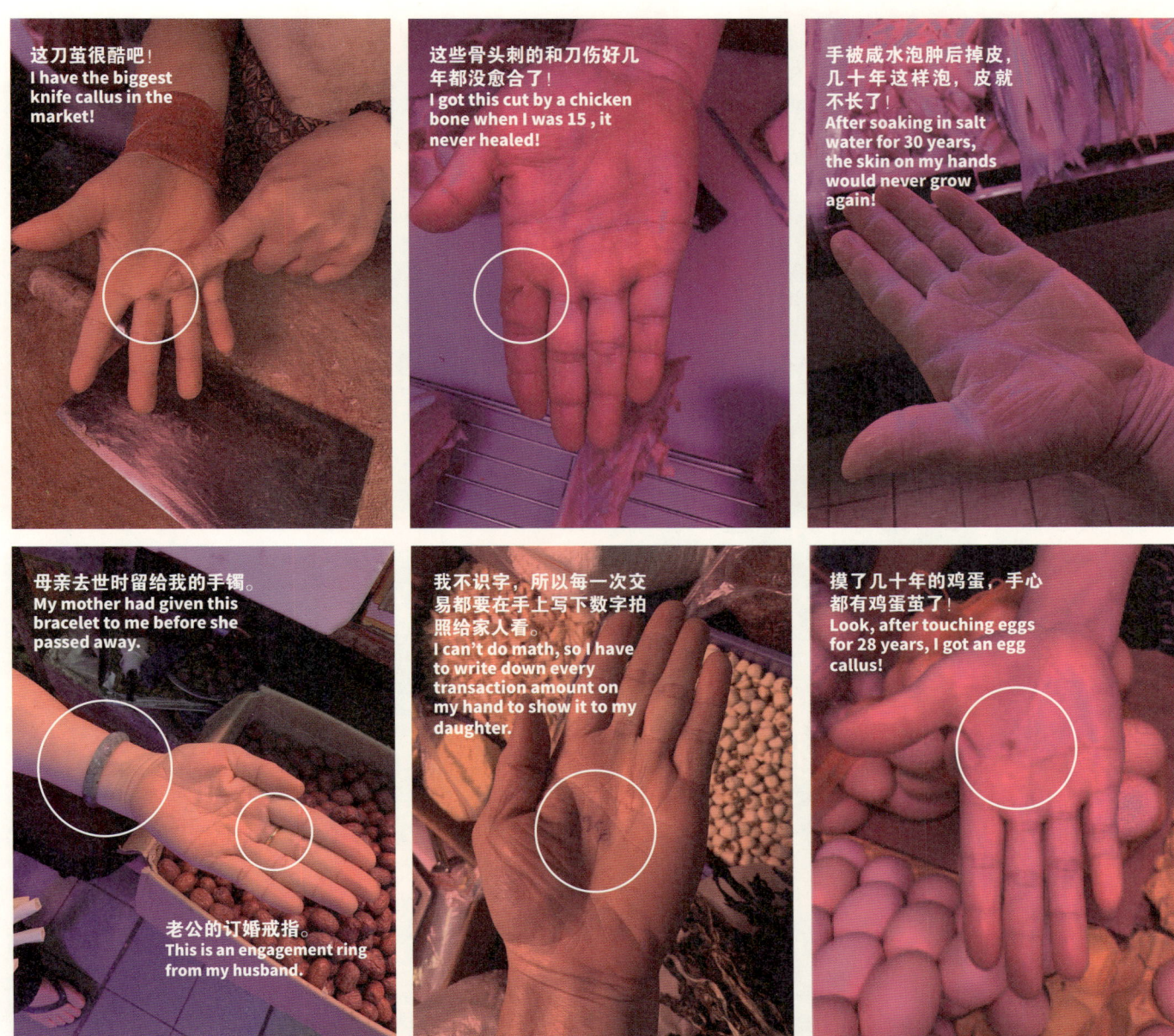

手的故事
摊主们终于接受学生和他们一起工作，并开始和学生分享他们的故事
The Stories of Hands
The vendors finally accepted the students to work with them and began to share their stories with the students

第一次参观
2018 年 5 月 28 日，菜市场的摊贩们 11 年以来第一次参观一墙之隔的美术馆
First Visit
On 28 May 2018, the next-door vendors paid their first visit to the museum in 11 years

记录摊贩们的手
学生们为 44 位摊贩的手拍照，作为工作坊最后的"改造"成果
Recording Vendors' Hands
The students took photos of 44 vendors' hands as the result of "transformation" conducted by the workshop

双手的照片被摊贩挂在了他们的营业执照旁边
The vendors hung photos of their hands next to their business licenses

联接的媒介
通过双手，摊贩和当地居民开始在菜市场展开积极的对话

Hands as Agency of Connection
Through the medium of hands, positive dialogues between the vendors and the locals began to take place in the market

of all their happiness and the "asset" they are proudest of. So I asked my students to photograph the hands of all the vendors in the market.

2018年5月28日，作为工作坊作业汇报的展现形式，44位菜市场摊贩们的双手照片被学生高高挂在了"无界的墙"上面。正因为双手的照片，一墙之隔的摊贩11年来第一次踏入美术馆看展。展览结束后的第二天，所有摊贩再次来到美术馆，申请要回他们双手的照片，并自发在菜市场里策划了一场属于他们自己的"展览"——许多摊贩不约而同地把双手照片挂在了他们的营业执照旁边。和双手照片截然相反，营业执照是一个抽象和冰冷的行政符号，它只代表摊贩在这里经营的合法性。通过双手照片这个媒介，之前从未有过交流互动的摊贩和街坊之间开始相互关怀，他们之间的积极对话开始在菜市场里发生。双手照片以一种神奇的方式穿透坚硬的墙，将不同阶层和文化背景的人关联在一起，给予每个个体一份关爱和理解。

On 28 May 2018, as a format of the final exhibition of the workshop, the photographs of the vendors' hands were hung up by the students on the "Borderless Wall". Because of this exhibition, the next-door market vendors paid the first visit to the museum in 11 years. More surprisingly, the vendors collected the photographs of their hands after this exhibition and curated an "exhibition" of their own in the market. In a very ironic way, many vendors displayed the photographs of their hands next to their stall licenses. Contrary to the photos of hands, the business license is an abstract and cold administrative symbol, which only represents the legitimacy of the vendors' operation here. Through the medium of hands, the vendors and the locals started connecting with and caring for each other naturally, positive dialogues between them began to take place in the market. In a magic way, the "hands" penetrated the "hard wall" and became a bridge that connected people from different ranks and backgrounds, giving each individual caring and understanding.

在第一个工作坊结束之后，过去39年从未对菜市场产生过归属感的摊贩开始主导起菜市场的改造，甚至还成为社区改造的主角。2018年10月，一个名为"民众花园"的社区种植工作坊由扉美术馆发起，在更大范围内培育社区凝聚力。工作坊的学生号召社区每一位居民把家里闲置的日常容器（除了花盆以外的任何可以种植物的容器），贡献出来放在指定的社区公共空间。这些容器将被用于栽种植物，最终形成一个人人都可以参与种植的"民众花园"。出乎意料的是，最先开始行动的是菜市场的摊贩，从电视、马桶、行李箱、鞋子、电饭煲到小塑料瓶、易拉罐、碗等，摊贩们利用这些大小不一、材质和形状各异的容器种植的花草"盆栽"立即吸引了大量社区居民前来观看。几天后，受到摊贩影响的竹丝岗社区居民们带来了更多更大的"容器"，如废弃的浴缸、沙发、书柜和冰箱，并以非常富有想象力的方式与摊贩一起种植物，把这个曾经无人问津的场所变成了一个真正的民众的花园。

After the first workshop, the vendors began to take the ownership of their market and became the leading role of community transformations. In October 2018, another community-engaged workshop titled "People's Garden" was launched by the landscape architecture students to further foster community cohesion at a larger scale. The students called on everyone living in Zhusigang to donate a home container (anything containable except flower pots) to a designated site. The home containers from individuals then would be planted to form a community garden eventually. Unexpectedly, the market vendors made the first move to collect the containers, from abandoned televisions, closestools, suitcases, shoes and rice cookers to small plastic bottles, cans and bowls, and planted them on the site. These containers in various sizes, materials and shapes with flowers made by the vendors immediately attracted the local residents to come and participate. They even brought much larger home containers like disused bathtubs, sofas, book cases and fridges, and planted together with the vendors in very imaginative ways, transforming this once neglected place into a real people's garden.

为了建构一种主人翁意识和归属感，每个种有植物的"容器"上都放了一个有种植者名字的标签。当个人的情感和记忆被注入到这座花园时，不同背景和社会阶层的人群开始每天聚集在这里，不同的意见、情感、文化、思想、故事、价值观、知识和信息在这里相互交换和碰撞。于是，"民众花园"变成了一个真正由民众自己建造，并为民众服务的花园。"民众花园"这个理念不仅扩展了容器已有的用途，很好地阐述了"物尽其用"的意义，而且还重新定义了公

菜市场摊贩的参与
2018年11月26日，菜场摊贩最先把收集来的旧电视机、行李箱、鞋子、电饭煲、小塑料瓶、易拉罐、碗等容器拉到指定场地，并在现场种植

Participation of Market Vendors
On November 26, 2018, the market vendors took the initiative to carry the collected containers, ranging from abandoned televisions, suitcases, shoes and rice cookers to small plastic bottles, cans and bowls, to the designated place and planted on the site

"民众花园"的形成
受到摊主们的启发和影响，竹丝岗社区居民也慢慢参与进来，以非常富有想象力的方式把这个空间变成了一个民众自建的花园

The Formation of "People's Garden"
Inspired and influenced by the vendors, the local residents began to plant in various kinds of containers in very imaginative ways, which gradually transformed this site into a garden built by people

129

人民城市人民建
为了在人们心中建立创造一种主人翁意识和归属感，每一个种了植物的容器都贴上了种植者的名字

People's City Built by People
To create a sense of ownership and belonging in people's hearts, every planted container was labelled with the planter's name

"民众花园"的社交聚会
菜市场摊贩和社区居民第一次在"民众花园"聚会

Social Gatherings in "People's Garden"
The market vendors and the local residents had their first gathering in "People's Garden"

共空间的概念。更重要的是，这个项目让不同阶层和背景的人们能够参与到城市空间"公共性"的建构中来，成为公共空间的主导者和创造者。

In order to create a sense of ownership and belonging, every planted container was labelled with the planter's name. When individual emotions and memories were injected into this garden, people, regardless of their backgrounds and social classes, started gathering together here every day and exchanged opinions, emotions, cultures, thoughts, stories, values, knowledge and information. People's Garden was truly created by the people and for the people, which not only extended the use of a container but also redefined the notion of "public space". More importantly, this project empowered the public to participate and engage in the making of public space in their communities.

遗憾的是，由于其看似杂乱无章的形象，"民众花园"在建成后不久就被相关部门清除了。然而，"民众花园"却让菜市场摊贩和当地居民之间建立了更为紧密的联系。2019年12月，摊贩向美术馆提出，在菜市场承办一年一度的"百家宴"，并邀请竹丝岗社区居民到菜市场和他们一起打边炉，庆祝新的一年的到来。

Sadly, People's Garden was cleaned up not long after its completion by the local authority due to its anarchic presence. However, the People's Garden project created a stronger bond between the vendors and the locals. In December 2019, the vendors took the initiative in hosting the annual "hundred-family banquet", inviting the local residents to dine together in their market.

在过去的三年里，摊贩一直在问我一个问题："作为一名建筑师，你为什么不去设计房子，而是和我们一起在市场里瞎闹？"其实，在这个项目里，我所指向的"建筑"不是一个消极被动的名词，比如一栋房子，而是一种人与人之间、人与社会之间关联和共情的重新连接，一种新的积极的社会关系的建构，一个行动和动员的词汇。在这个理解下，"菜市场美术馆"项目就是一个建筑的过程。

In the past three years, the vendors have been asking me a question: "As an architect, why don't you go design houses instead of hanging around with us in the market?" In fact, in this project, the "architecture" I refer to is not a passive noun, such as a house, but a reconnection of relation and empathy between people as well as people and society; a construction of new positive social relations; and a word of action and mobilization. In this understanding, the "Market Museum" project is a process of "architecture".

参与式设计研讨会
学生们在菜市场中与摊贩并肩工作（左）；
学生们与摊贩、市场的业主、街道工作人员和社区居民开会讨论菜市场的改造（右）

Participatory Community Workshop
The students working with the vendors side by side in the market (left);
The students having a meeting with the vendors, the market owners, the government officials and the local residents to discuss the market's future (right)

2019年8月4日,扉美术馆在农林菜市场和"无界的墙"上开窗
On August 4, 2019, a window was opened on the wall of the Nonglin Market and "Borderless Wall"

《汗》——菜市场摊主阿正与扉美术馆的第一件作品
Sweat — the first work of vendor Azheng and FEI Arts

2019 年 8 月，窗口慢慢成为一个网红打卡点
The window was gradually turned into an "Instagram Hotspot" in August 2019

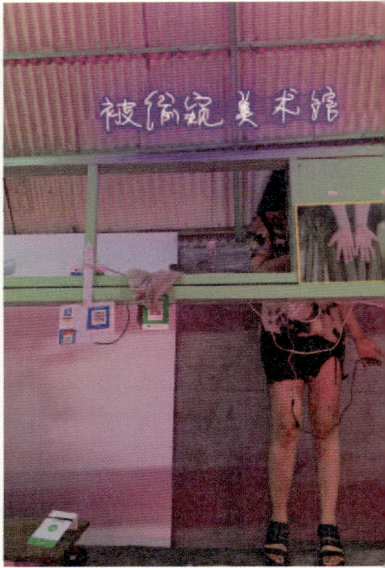

《被偷窥美术馆》——摊主阿正与美术馆合作的第二件作品。2019年8月11日，阿正一天卖出去了120瓶矿泉水，挣了420元

An Art Museum Being Peeped by the Public—the second work jointly created by the vendor Azheng and FEI Arts. On August 11, 2019, Azheng sold 120 bottles of mineral water and earned RMB 420

137

2020年10月,因菜市场的拆迁,阿正离开广州,并带走了他与扉美术馆合作的灯牌作品
In October 2020, when Azheng left Guangzhou owing to the demolition of the market, he took away the led signboard that he co-created with FEI Arts

与某些被资本与权力主导的社区营造行为不一样的是,这个项目没有把菜市场变成一个网红打卡点,也完全没有触碰菜市场看似破旧不堪的物理空间,而是通过一系列极其柔软的介入甚至是不造物的方式来重新构建摊贩生而为人的尊严和自信,在此基础上唤醒大众日益消逝的集体意识和对公共空间的主导意识,并将之转化为今天中国城市更新和社区营造最重要的一股力量。

Unlike some community transformation practices dominated by capital and power, this project does not turn the market into an internet-famous site, neither does it touch the seemingly dilapidated physical space of the market at all, but reconstructs the dignity and self-confidence of the vendors through a series of extremely soft interventions or even non-creative ways, on the basis of which, it awakens the public to the fading sense of collectiveness and ownership over community, and turn it into the most critical force behind the ongoing urban renewal and community empowerment across China today.

市场里的"百家宴"
2019 年 12 月 7 日,摊贩们主动举办了一年一度的"百家宴",邀请当地居民在市场里聚餐
"Hundred-Family Banquet" in the Market
On December 7, 2019, the vendors voluntarily hosted the annual "hundred-family banquet", and invited the local residents to dine together in the market

2020年10月20日,农林菜市场被拆除
On October 20, 2020, the Nonglin Market was demolished

美术馆里的菜市场
A Market in the Museum

2020 年 12 月 5 日，豆腐档档主祁红艳终于在附近汤料店的一个角落找到了一个摊位

On December 5, 2020, Qi Hongyan, a tofu vendor, finally secured a corner in a nearby soup ingredients shop to set up her stall

2020 年 10 月 20 日，经营了 39 年的农林菜市场因违建和环境原因被有关部门责令拆除。根据城市发展的要求，农林菜市场将被一个社区花园取代，而菜市场的 44 位摊贩另寻他处，继续摆摊谋生。

On October 20, 2020, the Nonglin Market, which had been in operation for 39 years, was ordered to be demolished by the local authorities for illegal construction and environmental reasons. According to the requirements of urban development, the market would be replaced by a community garden, and the 44 vendors working there would go somewhere else to set up their stalls to make a living.

2021 年 4 月 30 日，豆腐摊贩担心《豆腐美术馆》灯牌被晒着，撑了一把小伞挡着
On April 30, 2021, the tofu vendors held up a small umbrella to protect the led logo sign of *Tofu Art Museum* from the sun

当"轰隆隆"的挖掘机摧毁农林菜市场的时候，流落于附近街头的摊贩们不约而同在各自的摊位上挂起了自己双手的照片，以示控诉。望着这个情景，我的心情不觉沉重起来。这种沉重不仅来自对这个群体苦难的共情，还源于长久以来在强大的结构面前产生的痛楚和深深的无力感。在城市发展不可阻挡的浪潮中，农林菜市场的 44 位摊贩就像是 44 朵无足轻重的浪花，在菜市场轰然倒塌的那一刻，他们被溅洒得无影无踪，似乎从来没存在过一样，连同名字一起也被人们遗忘了。他们当中，有独自在菜市场卖鸡肉 32 年，养活一家四口的湖南岳阳人郑爱萍；有从童工开始做起，然后把弟弟和弟媳妇一起带到菜市场卖冻肉的广东云浮人岑秋颜；有 12 年前为照顾生病的家人，辞掉公司文职在菜市场卖菜的陕西西安人郭文正；还有在菜市场卖豆腐 28 年从未回过老家，只盼着在广州有个容身之地再衣锦还乡的安徽马鞍山人祁红艳……

As the rumbling excavator was demolishing the market, the vendors who scattered around the nearby streets hung the pictures of their hands over stalls to express their anger. The sight of this scene made my heart heavy. Such heaviness came not only from the empathy for the suffering group, but also from the pain and deep sense of helplessness that has long been generated in the face of the powerful structure. In the irresistible tide of urban development, the 44 vendors of Nonglin Market were like 44 insignificant spoondrifts. At the moment when the market collapsed, they were splashed without a trace left, as if they had never existed, and were forgotten together with their names. Among them, Zheng Aiping, a native of Yueyang, Hunan Province, has been selling chicken in the market alone for 32 years to feed a family of four; Cen Qiuyan, a native of Yunfu, Guangdong Province, started as a child laborer and then brought her brother and sister-in-law to the market to sell frozen meat; Guo Wenzheng, a native of Xi'an, Shaanxi Province, gave up her office job in a company 12 years ago to take care of his sick family members and sell vegetables in the market; and Qi Hongyan, a native of Ma'anshan, Anhui Province, has been selling tofu in the market for 28 years and never returned to her hometown, hoping to secure a place of her own in Guangzhou before returning to hometown in full glory...

导演贾樟柯说，当一个社会急匆匆往前赶路的时候，不能因为要往前走，就忽视那个被你撞倒的人。我知道，不只是那 44 位失去菜市场的摊贩，我们每一个人都有可能成为那个被撞倒、被无视的人。半年之后，策展人冯博一邀请我参加他在重庆悦来美术馆策划的一个名为"向下生活里的 X 种空间方案"的建筑展，并建议我可以通过这个展览对农林菜市场的消失做一个回应。于是，我想到了在美术馆里重建农林菜市场。对我来说，纵使失去无力挽回，记录与重建本身就是一种对抗。但实现这个愿望，并不是我一个人的事情，还需要有更多认同此次"重建"的人一起参与进来。于是，我决定发起一次众筹与那些和我怀着相同愿望的人，为44位摊贩，也为我们自己"重建"一座农林菜市场。

The Chinese film director Jia Zhangke said that when the society rushes forward, it shouldn't ignore the people it knocked down just because it wants to go forward. I know that it's not just about the 44 vendors who lost the market, actually every one of us could be the one who gets hit and ignored. Half a year later, the curator Feng Boyi invited me to participate in an architectural exhibition entitled "X Kinds of Space Schemes in Downward Life" curated by him at Yuelai Art Museum in Chongqing, and suggested that I could respond to the disappearance of Nonglin Market through this exhibition. Therefore, I thought of "rebuilding" the market in the art gallery. For me, even if the loss can't be restored, the recording and rebuilding themselves would be a kind of confrontation. But making this happen is not just my own business, more people who agree with this idea of "rebuilding" need to join efforts. So I decided to launch a crowdfunding campaign to "rebuild" Nonglin Market for the 44 vendors, and also for ourselves, with people who have the same desire as mine.

第一次坐飞机的祁红艳和黄月香
Qi Hongyan and Huang Yuexiang were flying for the first time

共建者名单（按拼音顺序排列）/ Co-builder of Nonglin Market:
阿一、Alkali、蔡佳伶、蔡伊凡、曹劲、曹敏、苌大查、陈迪、陈佳佳、陈杰文、陈晶晶、陈晓露、陈欣仪、陈煊、陈竹、程大富、程谱章、橙医生、大若、戴天树、邓小姐、邓阳、刁珊、丁曼文、丁鹏、董顺丹、杜亚琳、樊女士、范久江、方蔼珈、方霖、飞扬、费双、冯博一、付毅兵、甘嘉升、高冬阳、高玥、葛宇路、宫柏馨、古多吉、关雷、关鸣、关颖茵、桂颖、郭佳灵、郭兰都、郭耀慧、韩雪、韩易珊、韩玉龙、郝家齐、何凯晶、何思岑、何韦萱、何欣、何渝、何志森、侯振海、胡金池、胡茜、胡晓雯、胡泽浩、胡志伟、黄彬凌、黄活、黄家安、黄靖欣、黄漫浠、黄诗云、黄文莉、黄心怡、黄雨欣（佛山）、黄雨欣（张家界）、黄月香、黄子倪、黄子为、Jack Lai、家望、贾铠针、贾欣悦、姜虹羽、姜宇霏、蒋少武、金、九姑娘、柯亦坤、孔玉仪、旷宇、蓝莉瑶、黎思娆、李波、李淳毅、李聪毅、李迪华、李甫、李耕、李涵、李寒、李惠枚、李佳、李金洁、李俊荣、李梁、李敏稚、李平、李思欣、李晓彤、李啸、李抒欣、梁晓帆、廖若星、林大海、林钿、林广思、林俊、林世华、林双华、林文警、林欣、林欣祺、凌晓红、刘超、刘二囍、刘飞林、刘先森、刘学兰、刘逸安、刘悦来、柳佰春、龙艾、龙天音、卢嘉鑫、卢远良、卢泽达、陆柯萍、鹿禄、罗曼莹、罗仕鹏、罗添茂、罗颖、骆红亚、Monimobi、马岱涵、马倩雅、马小芳、马智健、麦小新、毛恺琳、米笑、莫莹、莫子皓、年子范、欧蓝晰、庞庄庄、彭琬玲、彭雪莹、祁红艳、钱敏燕、全兴平、冉峡、阮化英、阮欣、撒莹、山妖、佘佳俐、申通、沈佶、沈素霞、沈煜、时静洁、宋冬、孙念念、孙社瑜、孙一民、Taya、台尧、唐丹璇、田雨婷、袜子、汪益民、王斌斌、王翠红、王宁、王秋月、王珊、王申、王晓松、王新、王亚冠、王爷、魏青兰、魏晓彤、文那、巫晓晖、吴琛、吴双、吴文媛、吴晓叶、吴阳秋、吴元梓、夏光、肖菊、肖敏、谢佳、谢谨阳、谢琳、谢汶雨、熊楷、熊真、修曦宇、徐碧穗、徐婵娟、徐佳、徐姐、徐腾、徐运林、许自力、薛璇、薛源、言冬、杨丽歆、杨亚非、杨一丁、杨艺涛、杨雨雯、叶木森、叶谢谢、叶叶、叶子、尤舒蓉、游天龙、于悦、袁源、岳阳、张冰、张持、张岱霓、张夸夸、张兰花、张杏儿、张宁（北京）、张宁（深圳）、张萍、张诗洋、张维、张欢、张霄、张新烨、张寅、张宇、章嵘、招媛谊、昭禾王、赵翠云、赵沐、赵青、赵忠诚、郑爱萍、郑嘉骏、郑晶、郑敏澄、郑庆龄、钟冠球、周国欢、周立、周倩玲、朱骞、曾帆、曾佳阳、曾令婕、曾颖

悦来美术馆 5 号厅展墙上 300 位共建者名单

List of 300 co-builders on the exhibition wall of No.5 Hall of Yue Lai Art Museum

农林市场欢迎您　何志森

农林菜市场坐落于广州东山口竹丝岗社区
在过去的三年,我带领学生在农林菜市场种
改造和艺术创作项目。2020 年 10 月 20 日
市场因违建原因被有关部门责令拆除,44
求,农林菜市场将被一个社区花园所取代
加他在重庆悦来美术馆策划的一个建筑展
菜市场的消失做一个回应。于是,我想到了
……
我知道,无论怎样的"重建",都改变不了
了此刻正流落于街头的摊贩们所遭受的艰
这样一个高雅华贵的艺术殿堂里重建一个
贩一个本该有却从未获得的尊重和礼遇
……
感谢每一位农林菜市场的共建者,是你让

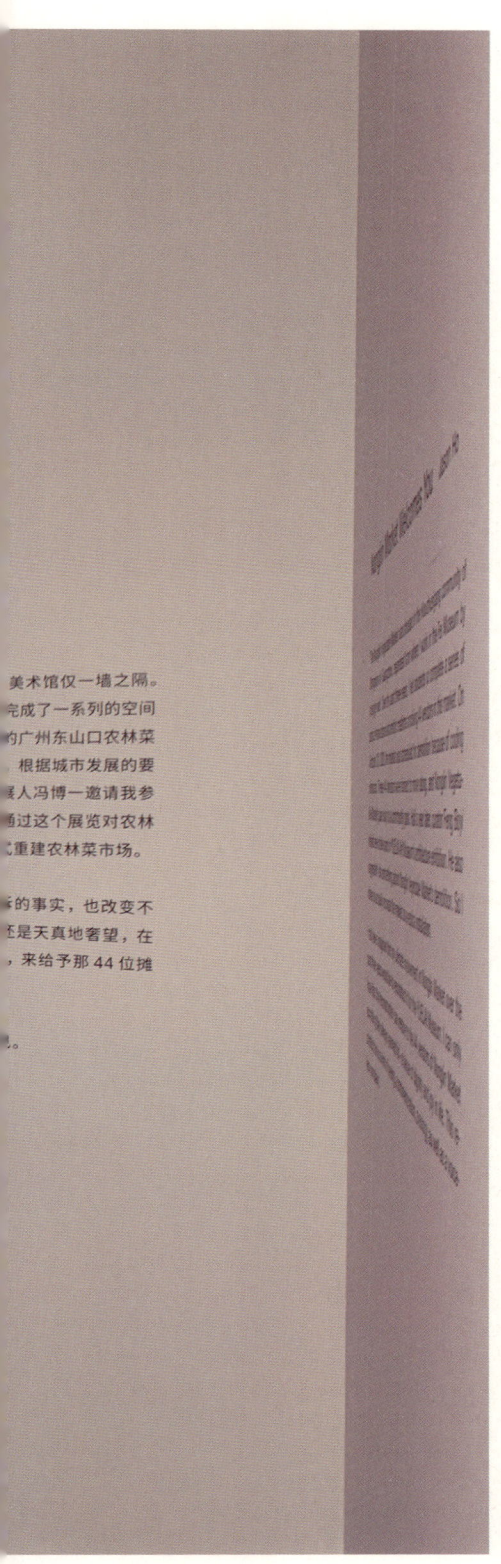

当我把要在美术馆重建农林菜市场的消息告诉摊贩们的时候,他们没有流露出一丝的喜悦,反而质问我:"你在美术馆盖菜市场和我们有什么关系?我们还不是天天照样被城管赶?有谁会在乎我们?"我知道,无论怎样的"重建",都改变不了此刻正流落于街头的摊贩们所遭受的艰辛和无助。因此,我心里非常清楚,在美术馆重建菜市场的意义不只是为了还原某个消失的空间场景,更重要的是去致敬39年来那些在农林菜市场悄无声息用尽全力活着的人们。我希望在这样一个如此高雅华贵的艺术殿堂里重建一个被拆的菜市场,来给予那44位摊贩一个本该有却从未获得的尊重和礼遇。

When I told the vendors that I was going to rebuild Nonglin Market in the gallery, they did not show even the slightest joy, but asked me: "What does it have to do with us if you build a market in the gallery? Aren't we still being driven away by the city inspectors every day? Who cares about us?" I know that no matter what kind of "rebuilding" it is, it would not relieve the hardship and helplessness of the vendors who are tramping the streets now. Therefore, I am very clear that the significance of rebuilding the market in the art gallery is not only to restore a lost space scene, but also to pay tribute to the people who have been silent and tried to survive at Nonglin Market for 39 years. I wish to rebuild a demolished market in such an elegant and luxurious art palace to give the 44 vendors respect and courtesy that they deserve but never received.

2021年7月3日下午2点45分,距展览开幕不到1个小时,悦来美术馆5号展厅"农林市场欢迎您"作品的音频设备刚刚安装完毕,空旷的展厅里响起了8个月前农林菜市场熟悉的吵闹声。这段仅有14分55秒的背景声音录制于2020年10月19日下午3点至4点,收录了菜市场关闭前6小时我和44位摊主之间的告别。我在展厅里来来回回地走着,忐忑不安地等待着两个人的到来——她们是从广州专程赶来重庆参加展览开幕的原农林菜市场摊主祁红艳和黄月香。

At 2:45 pm on July 3, 2021, less than an hour before the opening of the exhibition, the audio equipment for the works of "Nonglin Market Welcomes You" in Yuelai Art Museum had just been installed, and the familiar noise of Nonglin Market finally sounded in the empty exhibition hall. Recorded between 3 pm and 4 pm on October

"农林市场欢迎您"展览入口处
The entrance of "Welcome to Nonglin Market" exhibition

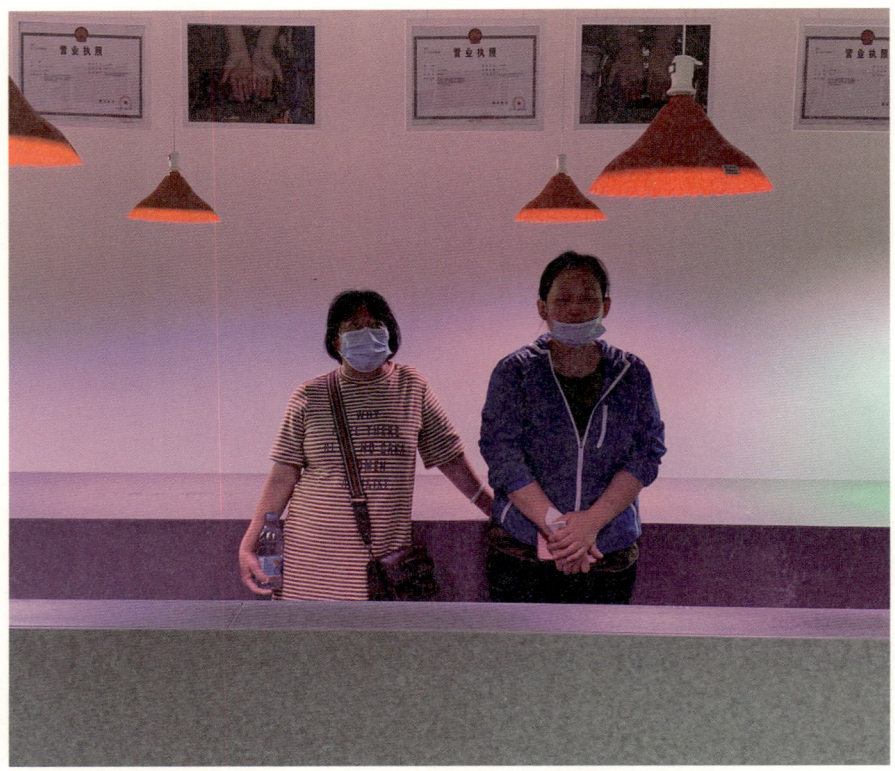

祁红艳和黄月香在自己的档口前
Qi Hongyan and Huang Yuexiang in front of their stalls

19, 2020, the 14 minutes and 55 seconds of background sound captures the farewell between me and 44 vendors six hours before the market's closure. I walked back and forth in the exhibition hall, nervously waiting for the arrival of two important people, Qi Hongyan and Huang Yuexiang, former vendors of Nonglin Market who came all the way from Guangzhou to Chongqing to attend the opening of the exhibition.

对于重建农林菜市场这件作品，从开始策划到展览开幕前的最后一刻，我都一直处在一种自我怀疑的状态之中。当策展人冯博一邀请我参展并问我能否对菜市场的拆除做一个回应的时候，我的内心是不确定的。如果我连摊主们最基本的工作权益都争取不了，那做这展览还有什么意义？在我看来，无论做什么作品，无论这件作品有多么深远的意义，农林菜市场的拆除和44位摊主的遭遇都只会成为我作品的一个创作素材和背景而已。因此，我完全不敢想象，当两位摊主怀揣着农林菜市场被重建的希望，最终看到的却是一个不能摆摊、仅供人拍照欣赏的"菜市场"时内心的失落。

From the beginning of planning to the last moment before the opening of the exhibition, I have been in a state of self-doubt about the rebuilding of Nonglin Market. When curator Feng Boyi invited me to participate in the exhibition and asked if I could respond to the demolition of the market, I was uncertain at heart. If I can't fight for the most basic working rights of the vendors, what's the point doing this exhibition? To me, whatever works I could make and no matter how far-reaching their significance may be, the demolition of Nonglin Market and the experiences of the 44 vendors would only become source and background for my creation. Therefore, I dare not imagine the deep disappointment of the two vendors who, holding the hope for a rebuilding of Nonglin Market, finally see a "market" that cannot be set up, but only to be photographed and viewed.

3点15分，祁红艳怀抱着她刚满月不久的小儿子康康、黄月香以及她女儿黄文莉走进了悦来美术馆，此时的她们还不知道即将面对的是怎样的一个场景。踏入5号展厅的那一刻，看到已经消失8个月的农林菜市场的还原场景，黄月香和祁红艳并没有说一句话。黄月香首先认出了自己双手的照片，骄傲地对祁红艳说："呐，这个手是我的！" 但当黄月香看到自己的名字被雕刻在"档口"台面上的时候，她开始变得激动起来，她万万没有想到每一个摊主的名字竟然会以这样的方式被大家看见。在过去的39年，没有人知道他们的名字，即便在菜市场被拆除之后，他们也没有被记住。

At 3:15 pm, when Qi Hongyan, holding her youngest son, the one-month-old baby boy Kangkang in her arms, walked into Yuelai Art Museum, together with Huang Yuexiang and her daughter Huang Wenli, they had no idea what kind of scene they were about to face. The moment they stepped into exhibition hall and saw the restored scene of Nonglin Market that had disappeared for 8 months, Huang and Qi did not say a word. Huang first recognized the photo of her hands and proudly said to Qi: "Wow, these hands are mine!" When Huang saw her name carved on the "stall" table, she became so excited. She didn't have the least expectation that every vendor's name would be seen in such a way. In the past 39 years, no one knew their names; even after the market was demolished, they have not been remembered.

与颇为激动的黄月香相比，祁红艳全程几乎没有说一个字。再次面对这样熟悉却陌生的场景，她显得有点不知所措。在菜市场消失8个月后，祁红艳第一次听到摊主们亲切的声音，她的眼圈开始泛红。祁红艳后来告诉我，菜市场消失之后，她以为她这辈子再也听不到这些声音了。她说："就好像你失去了一位很亲很亲的人，有一天你突然再次听到他的声音，但你知道他再也不会出现了，这是惊喜还是悲伤，我也无法说清楚。"

Compared with the rather excited Huang, Qi hardly said a word throughout the whole journey. Faced with such a familiar but strange scene again, she seemed a bit at a loss. Eight months after the disappearance of Nonglin Market, Qi heard the friendly voices of the vendors for the first time, and her eyes began to turn wet. Qi later told me that after the market disappeared, she thought she would never hear these voices again in her life. She said: "It's like you've lost someone very very dear to you, and one day you suddenly hear his voice again, but you know he's never coming back. Whether it's surprise or sadness, I can't tell."

在祁红艳稍稍平静之后，她开始拿起手机对着每个档口台面上的名字一边拍视频，一边大声念出每一位摊主的名字，然后把这些视频发到了"市场一家人"微信群里——这是他们在菜市场拆除之后为了便于联络建的一个群。一些不明真相的摊主们看到这些视频之后，开始纷纷在群里给祁红艳留言："豆腐（祁红艳的别称），农林菜市场是不是又建起来啦？可不可以帮我留一个档口？""豆腐，这是在哪里？我们马上过来！""豆腐，为什么没有我的名字？"……一时间，"市场一家人"群里炸开了锅。

After Qi calmed down a little bit, she began to use her mobile phone to take videos of the names on the counter of each stall, reading out the names of each vendor, and then sent the videos to the "Market Family" WeChat group, which they set up to facilitate communication after the demolition of the market. After seeing these videos, some vendors who did not know the truth began to leave messages for Qi in the group: "Qi, is Nonglin Market built again? Can you help reserve a stall for me?" "Qi, where is this? We'll be right there！" "Qi, why isn't my name there？"...For a time, the "Market Family" WeChat group exploded.

由于悦来美术馆的 5 号展厅面积比农林菜市场小一半，为了尽量还原空间的真实性，我没有把所有的档口都放进去。当祁红艳知道并不是所有人的档口都在的时候，她的脸上流露出了一丝的悲伤。"我们都像亲人一样，希望大家都可以一直一起，缺了谁都不完整……"祁红艳还没说完，我便接到原农林菜市场蔬菜摊摊主邓贤梅的电话："何老师，农林菜市场是不是又开张了？可不可以帮我留一个档口呀？我随时都可以开工。"听着电话那头邓贤梅激动的声音，我突然一阵心酸，我不知道该怎么回答。

祁红艳触摸雕刻在"档口"上的名字

Qi Hongyan touched the name carved on the "stall"

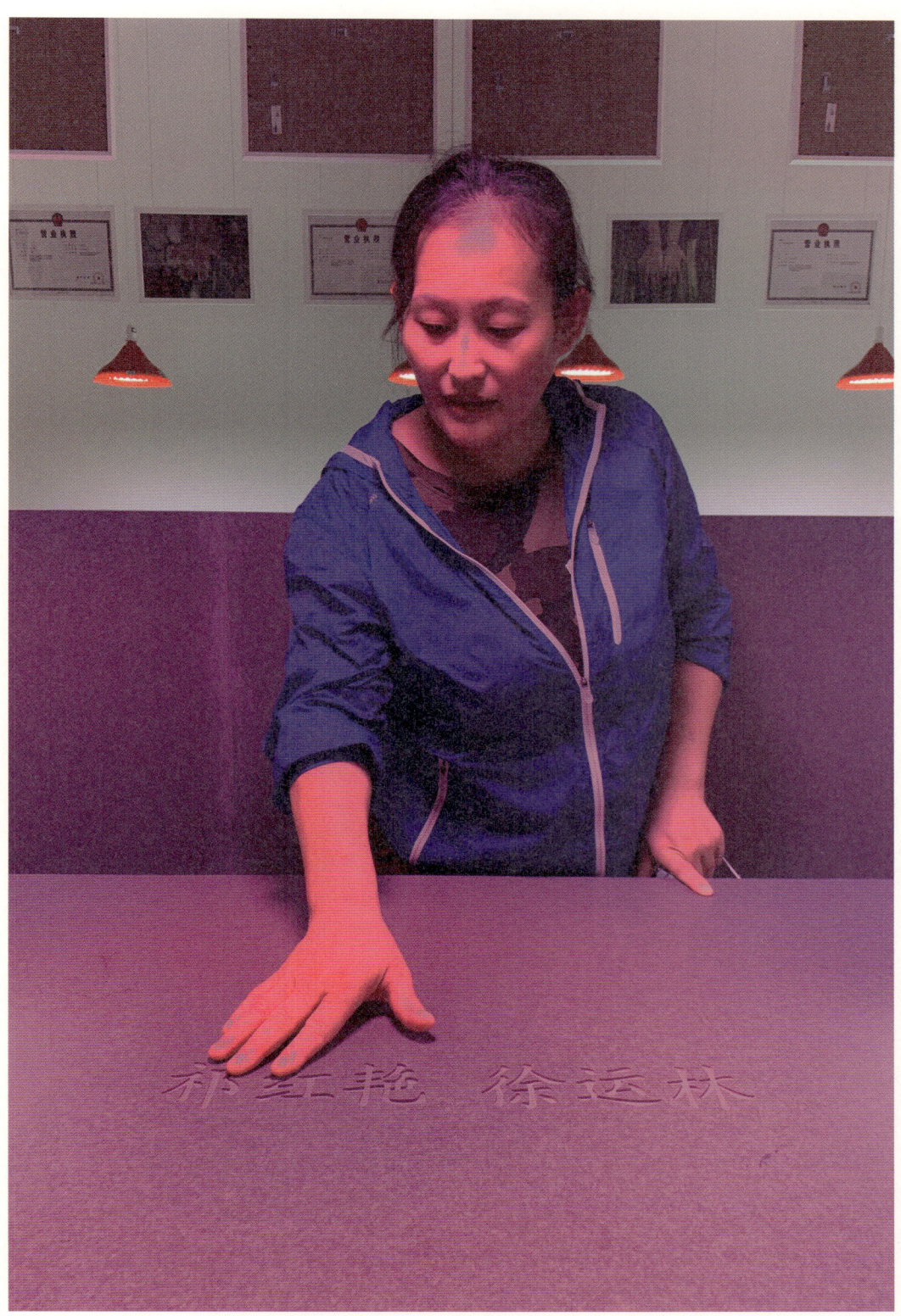

Because the given exhibition space of Yuelai Art Museum was half smaller than Nonglin Market, in order to restore the authenticity of the space as far as possible, I did not put all the stalls in. When Qi realized that not everyone's stalls were there, her face showed a trace of sadness. "We are like a family. I hope all of us can always be together. Whoever is missing, the family is incomplete…" Hardly had Qi finished when I received a phone call from Deng Xianmei, the former vegetable vendor of Nonglin Market: "Jason, is Nonglin Market open again? Can you help reserve a stall for me? I can start work at any time." The excited voice of Deng on the other end of the phone shot a sudden pang of sadness through my heart and I didn't know how to respond.

当走到自己的档口面前的时候，祁红艳突然问我可不可以爬进去，她想和小儿子康康一起照一张相留念。康康是在菜市场拆除之后不久出生的，他连妈妈的档口长什么样都没见过。祁红艳站在档口里，笑着对着怀里的孩子说："康康，这是妈妈曾经在广州的容身之地，虽然连一平方米都没有，但我们都很满足了。"对于祁红艳来说，和安徽农村老家的赤贫相比，能在农林菜市场拥有这样一个小小的档口就象征着某种成功，至少她的半只脚已经踏进了这座现代化的大都市。而农林菜市场的突然消失，让一家人又回到了一无所有的起点。

When reaching her stall, Qi suddenly asked me if she could climb in. She wanted to take a picture with her youngest son Kangkang there. Kangkang was born shortly after the demolition of the market, and he had never seen what his mother's stall looked like. Qi stood inside the stall, smiling at the baby in her arms and said: "Kangkang, this is the place where your mother used to work in Guangzhou. Although it's less than one square meter, we are very satisfied." For Qi, compared with the abject poverty in her countryside hometown in Anhui, having such a small stall at Nonglin Market symbolizes some kind of success for at least one foot of hers has stepped into the modern metropolis. However, the sudden disappearance of the market has brought the family back to the starting point of down-and-out.

在 44 面空白的锦旗墙面前，黄月香问我："何老师，这些旗子都没字的吗？"面对黄月香的问题，那种熟悉的无力感再次向我袭来，我不知道该如何与她解释这件作品的含义。无字锦旗所被赋予的意义与锦旗本该承担的"感谢"背道而驰，它们被叠加在一起悬挂在墙上，营造的是一种无声的控诉。这 44 面锦旗代表着农林菜市场的 44 位摊主，在农林菜市场被拆之后，为城市发展做出退让的他们连一句最基本的"谢谢"都没有得到。

原农林菜市场豆腐摊摊主祁红艳在悦来美术馆为看展的观众讲解作品
Qi Hongyan, the former tofu stall owner of the Nonglin market, explained the works to the audience at the Yuelai Art Museum

在悦来美术馆重建的农林菜市场
The Nonglin Market rebuilt in the Yuelai Art Museum

In front of the wall with 44 blank thank-you flags, Huang asked me: "Jason, are these flags without words?" Facing this question, the familiar feeling of helplessness drowned me again. I didn't know how to explain the meaning of this work to her. The meaning given by the wordless flags is contrary to the "gratitude" that a thank-you flag should bear, and they are superimposed on the wall to create a silent accusation. The 44 flags represent the 44 stall owners of the Nonglin Market. After the market was demolished, they did not even get the most basic thank you for making concessions for urban development.

离开重庆的时候，黄月香开玩笑说："摊位两天都没人看着，不知道城管会不会把东西都收走了？"在这个标榜着"城市让生活更美好"的时代，这一群安分守己、天性善良的摊贩们却从未被时代眷顾，即便他们时时刻刻都在期盼着有一天可以融入这座城市，成为"美好生活"的一部分。他们拼尽了全力寻得的机会却根本无法帮他们抵挡生活中不断被冒犯的危险，甚至他们连区区一平方米的生存空间都要为城市高歌猛进的发展让路。

Huang joked when she left Chongqing: "No one watched over our stalls for two days. I don't know whether or not the city inspectors have taken everything away." In an era boasting of "City makes life better", this group of law-abiding and good-natured vendors have never been favored by the times, though they always look forward to being integrated into the city one day and becoming part of the better life. They have tried their best to find opportunities, but still can't resist various kinds of risks constantly cropping up in life; even their one-square-meter working space had to make way for the rapid development of the city.

生活依然继续，黄月香和祁红艳，还有剩余的42位摊主的命运并没有因为重庆这个展览而发生一丝的改变。为了弥补因去重庆而两天未出摊的损失，黄月香和祁红艳回到广州后直接拖著行李奔向她们摆摊的街头，那里有等着她们开档的摊位。

Life still goes on, the fate of Huang Yuexiang and Qi Hongyan as well as the remaining 42 vendors, has not changed a bit because of this exhibition in Chongqing. In order to make up for the two days loss of vending business due to their Chongqing trip, upon returning to Guangzhou, Huang and Qi directly dragged their luggages to the street where there were stalls waiting for them to open.

44 副无字锦旗
44 wordless thank-you flags

离农林菜市场被拆过去整整 8 个月后，社区花园也已在菜市场的原址上悄悄建成，若没有花园上方那几片未拆掉的绿色铁架的提醒，几乎没有人会注意到这里曾经是一座经营了 39 年的菜市场。农林菜市场和 44 位摊主的命运，就像被海浪冲过的海滩，未留下一丝曾经存在的痕迹。

Now it has been 8 months since the Nonglin Market was demolished. A community garden has been quietly built on the original site of the market. Without the reminder of the green iron frame above the garden, one would hardly notice that this was once a market that had been in operation for 39 years. The fate of Nonglin Market and its 44 vendors, like the beach washed by waves, didn't leave a trace of its existence.

"如果改变不了任何事，那这次重建有什么意义呢？"在我离开重庆那天，一位记者在电话里这样问我。我知道，我们不能寄托一个展览改变一群人的命运。但如果改变真的发生，也是因为有人看见了那些为城市发展让路却一无所有的人们正在遭遇什么。在我看来，看见是改变的前提，或许这就是此次展览的意义。

"What's the point rebuilding this market if it doesn't change anything?" On the day I left Chongqing, a reporter asked me over the phone. I know that we can't rely on a single exhibition to change the fate of a group of people. But if change does happen, it's also because someone has seen what happened to those who had nothing to their names but had to make way for urban development. In my understanding, seeing is the premise of change, and perhaps this is the significance of this exhibition.

如果说，过去的 4 年我在农林菜市场所做工作的意义是尝试重新唤醒摊贩们的自尊，那么在悦来美术馆，我则希望可以借助此次的重建，将摊贩内心深处一直以来渴望的东西——生而为人存在的权利，还给他们。对我来说，这种重建是一种看见、一种纪念、一种讴歌，更是一种无声的控诉。

If the significance of my work at the Nonglin Market in the past four years is to try to reawaken the self-esteem of the vendors, then at Yuelai Art Museum, I hope that with the rebuilding of Nonglin Market, I can return to the vendors what they have always longed for in their hearts—the right to exist as human beings. For me, this rebuilding is a kind of seeing, a kind of commemoration, a kind of eulogy, and furthermore, a kind of silent indictment.

农林菜市场关闭之前，2020 年 10 月
Before the closure of Nonglin Market in October 2020

在农林菜市场原址上建成的社区花园，2021 年 6 月
The community garden built on the original site of Nonglin Market, June 2021

不管怎样，农林菜市场的摊贩们并没有因为菜市场实体空间的消失而集体解散。他们抱团取暖、彼此依赖、相互关怀，继续在菜市场原址周边一起摆摊，共同生活。四年来"菜市场美术馆"这个项目协同各方力量努力重建的联结，延续至今。在访谈节目《十三邀》里，人类学家项飙说："个人尊严和意义的出路在于重新建构'附近'的关系，重新连接。"在 2020 年全球新冠肺炎疫情暴发之后，对城市断裂、社会关系、公共生活的重新关注，对"附近"正在消失的人和事的重新关注，是所有建筑师面临的一个最为艰巨的任务。

However, they set up their stalls around the original site of the market and live together, embracing, relying on and taking care of each other. The vendors as a collective didn't disappear along with the demolished market. Instead, the interpersonal connections that the "Market Museum" project managed to rebuild in the past four years has extended to this day. In the interview program *13 Invitation*, anthropologist Xiang Biao said:" the way out for one to gain personal dignity and meaning of life lies in reconstructing kind of 'vicinal' relationship and reconnecting." Since the outbreak of COVID-19 around the globe in 2020, it has become the most arduous task for all architects to recast their concerns over urban division, social relations, public life as well as the people and things that are disappearing in the "vicinity".

摊贩们在菜市场的废墟前举着他们的手的照片
The vendors holding a photo of their hands in front of the ruins of market

附录
Appendix

学术评论一
Academic Reviews 1

互联网时代的"社会冷凝器"——紫泥堂纤维板厂改造设计的意义

The "Social Condenser" in the Age of Internet—the Significance of Renovation of Zi Ni Tang Fiberboard Factory

汪原
Wang Yuan

华中科技大学建筑与城市规划学院

School of Architecture and Urban Planning, Huazhong University of Science and Technology

原文刊发于《建筑学报》2019 年 10 期,总第 613 期
The original article was published in the *Journal of Architecture*, No.10, 2019, Total No.613

摘 要

针对紫泥堂纤维板厂的改造设计与糖厂工业遗产场地的关联性、建筑空间逻辑与"斜杠青年"生活逻辑相互促发和形塑的关系,讨论分析了加厚边界的空间策略在改造设计中的具体运用。在肯定其改造设计所具有的空间实验性质的基础上,进一步分析了转化为社会实践的可能性。

Abstract

This paper aims to identify the relationships between the renovation design of Zi Ni Tang Fiberboard Workshop and the industrial heritage site of Sugar Factory, and the reciprocal enhancement between architectural spatial logic of the renovated factory and the logic of life of "slash youth", exploring how form is shaped due to reciprocity. It examines the application of the spatial strategy that thickens border in a renovation deign, and further analyzes the possibility of transforming the factory into social practice based on the confirmation of the renovation as a spatial experimentation.

关键词

社会冷凝器;斜杠青年;潜能分化;加厚边界

Keywords

social condenser; slash youth; potential differentiation; thickened boundary

紫泥堂纤维板厂改造设计给人的第一印象是有趣和生动的。有趣，是因为建筑师针对"斜杠青年"[1]这一互联网时代独特的群体，用空间叙事的方式，探讨了将他们的生活与工作状态向外展示的可能性；生动，是因为依据特定叙事逻辑组构而成的主体建筑的空间面向杂糅多姿。于是，人们不禁要问：这一生动有趣的改造设计是如何与巨大的工业遗产场地关联融通的？其空间逻辑与"斜杠青年"的生存逻辑是如何相互促发形塑的？是否具有空间实验的质性，并隐含进一步转化为社会实践的潜能等，这些都是值得深入探讨的问题。

I find the first impression of the renovation design of Zi Ni Tang Fiberboard Factory so interesting and vivid. It is interesting because the architect explores the possibility of showing the living and working conditions of the unique group of slash youth born in the Internet era[1] to the outside world in a way of space narrative. It is vivid because the space aspects of the main building, which is constructed based on specific narrative logic, is varied and colorful. Therefore, people may be tempted to ask: How does this vivid and interesting renovation design relate to the huge site of industrial heritage? How do its spatial logic and the survival logic of slash youth stimulate and shape each other? Moreover, whether it has the quality of space experiment and implies the potential of further transformation into social practice are also issues worthy of further discussion.

① 紫泥糖厂当年生产的情景
Production scene of the Zi Ni sugar factory in the past

1 被展示的工业遗产和当代生活方式
1 Industrial Heritage and Contemporary Lifestyle on Display

紫泥糖厂于1953年建成，初始生产规模是日榨1000吨甘蔗，到了1990年代，其产量已经达到了日榨4000吨，一跃成为华南地区最大的制糖厂。1998年，由于甘蔗销售价格低廉，蔗农不愿种植甘蔗，导致原料供量严重短缺而最终停产。

② 紫泥糖厂现在的状况
Current status of the Zi Ni sugar factory

The Zi Ni Sugar Factory was established in 1953, with an initial capacity to press 1000 tons of sugarcane per day. By 1990s, its capacity reached 4000 tons per day, making it the largest sugar factory in South China. In 1998, due to the low sales price of sugarcane, farmers were reluctant to plant sugarcane, resulting in a serious shortage of raw materials and eventually closedown of the factory.

糖厂主要生产区域占地180亩（12万平方米），其完整的配套设置相当于一个大型的社区。在当年火热的大工业生产中，糖厂不仅是这一区域工人劳动生产的中心，也是集体生活的中心。厂区高耸的烟囱和制糖车间巨型的空间，充分体现着劳动者精神上的统领性和集体主义的崇高性，甚至成为劳动者集体记忆的"圣地"。从当年大生产的火热，到近年的衰败和死寂，巨大的反差不仅凸显着因产业转型而导致的生产方式的变化，同时也意味着在去工业化的浪潮中，由工业生产所决定的统一协作的集体性生活方式的消失（图①、②）。

The main production area of the sugar factory covers an area of 180 mu (120,000 ㎡), and its complete supporting facilities are equivalent to a large community. In the peak years of industrial production, the factory was not only the center of labor production in this region, but also the center of collective life. The towering chimneys and the huge space of the sugar production workshop fully embodied the spiritual leadership in the workers and the nobility of collectivism, and even become a "holy place" in the workers' collective memory. From the hot production in those years to the decline and deadly silence in recent years, the huge contrast not only highlights the change of production mode caused by industrial transformation, but also implies the disappearance of the unified and cooperative collective life style determined by industrial production in the wave of de-industrialization (Figures ① and ②).

在近些年工业遗产改造的热潮中，凋敝10多年后的糖厂也迎来了转机。随着资本的进驻，在尚未对遗产价值进行评估和阐明的情况下，各种文化和艺术机构匆匆地置入当下的企图和未来的欲求，坦率地捏造着新的空间符号，致使原有依照制糖工艺而形成的整体空间呈现出碎片化状态（图③）。

In the upsurge of industrial heritage transformation in recent years, the sugar factory also ushered in a turning point over a decade after its downfall. With the investment of capital and absence of evaluation and clarification of the heritage value, various cultural and artistic institutions rushed in with attempts to interfere with the current and desires for the future, frankly fabricating new space symbols and resulting in the fragmentation of the overall space originally formed according to sugar making process (Figure ③).

此次改造的厂房在过去是生产纤维板的，是糖厂利用蔗渣进行多种生产经营的附属工厂。主体建筑是一个3层（层高6米、柱跨6米×8米）的机电控制室。由于机电和生产设备早已被拆卸变卖，建筑主体只剩下一个空壳。当把外围护墙体拆除后，实际上就是一个纯净的多米诺体系结构框架（图④）。

The workshop under renovation this time used to produce fiberboard and was one of the sugar plant's subsidiary factories using bagasse for diversified production and operation. The main building is a 3-storey electromechanical control room (with 6m f

③ 糖厂部分厂房改造后的情景
The scene after renovation of some workshops in the sugar factory

loor-to-floor height, 6m×8m column span). Since all the electromechanical and production equipment have already been dismantled and sold out, the main body of the building is just an empty shell. After the surrounding wall has been removed, it is actually a pure domino architecture framework (Figure ④).

改造的具体任务是要为6位互联网时代的"斜杠青年"量身定制可以融工作、家居、媒体发布、社交聚会等公共活动与私人生活为一体的高度混合空间。由于"斜杠青年"在多个领域涉足，所从事的工作希望有更高的社会关注度，因此他们的作品、产品，乃至工作方式和日常生活方式也都希望被展示出来，从而开启和引领一种有别于朝九晚五的全新的都市生活。

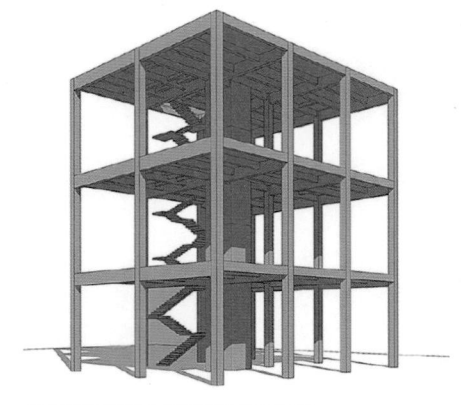

④ 纤维板厂机电控制室的结构框架
Structural framework of the electromechanical control room in the fiberboard workshop

The specific task of the transformation is to tailor a highly mixed space for six slash youths in the Internet era, integrating public activities (such as working, media conferencing, social gatherings) and private life. Since slash youths are involved in various fields and their work demands extensive social attention, they hope their works, products and even working methods and daily life styles can all be displayed, thus opening up and ushering in a new urban lifestyle different from the "9 am to 5 pm routine".

因此，这一改造设计就需要针对两种被展示的内容：其一，糖厂工业遗产独特的空间和生产工艺转化成的一种静态的工业景观；其二，"斜杠青年"特立独行的工作和生活方式。如何将两种需要被展示的内容有机地结合，从而成为一种文化产业而被社会消费，即是这个改造设计的核心。极为巧合的是建筑师本人也是涉足多个领域的"斜杠青年"，除了主持一个设计事务所，兼任广州扉美术馆的馆长，在设计各种与文创相关的项目的同时，还策划组织各类展览以及艺术活动。建筑师本人一直秉持的"无界"理念，以及以广州扉美术馆为基地所进行的一系列无界艺术社区介入活动，正好与"斜杠青年"职场和生活的无界感以及潜能分化的发展场域相契合。

Therefore, this renovation design needs to aim at two kinds of content for display: Firstly, a kind of static industrial landscape transformed from the unique space and the production craft of the Sugar Factory's industrial heritage; Secondly, the maverick work and lifestyle of "slash youth". How to combine the two kinds of content that need to be displayed organically, so as to make it a cultural industry to be consumed by the society, is the core of the renovation design. Coincidentally, the architect herself is also a slash youth involved in several fields. In addition to presiding over a design firm, she is also the curator of Guangzhou FEI Arts Museum; while designing various programs related to cultural creative projects, she also plans and organizes various exhibitions and artistic activities. The concept of "borderless" that the architect herself has always adhered to and a series of FEI Arts based intervention activities in borderless art community coincide with the borderless trait of career and life of "slash youth" as well as the development field of potential differentiation.

2 源自一幅漫画的空间原型
2 Space Archetype from a Cartoon

实际上，在一个既有的由梁板柱构成的抽象空间中置入不同的功能使用有其历史原型。早在100多年前，美国《生活》杂志(1909年3月)刊登的一幅对建筑领域影响至深的漫画即是始作俑者。该漫画由A.B.沃克创作，大标题是"在百老汇大街不到一英里的地方，用我们的钢材建造的精品地段，买一间舒适的小屋"。[1] 漫画描绘的是由钢结构建造的84层的摩天大楼，每一个水平层都被当作一个未开发的基地，围绕一幢乡村别墅及其马厩、仆人小屋等其他配套设施，建立一个完全独立的私人空间（图⑤）。

In fact, placing various functions in an existing abstract space composed of beams, slabs and columns, has its original archetype in history. As early as more than 100 years ago, the *Life* magazine (March 1909) of the USA published a cartoon which had a deep impact on the architecture field. The comic was produced by A.B. Walker and the headline was "Buy a cozy cottage in our steel constructed choice lots, less than a mile above Broadway". [1] The cartoon depicts an 84-storey skyscraper of steel structure, each level of which is used as an undeveloped base to establish a completely independent private space around a country house with amenities such as stables, servants' cabins and so on (Figure ⑤).

在沃克的这幅漫画发表70年之后，库哈斯对其进行了重新挖掘，并在其著作《癫狂的纽约》中进行更为深入的分析。库哈斯有意识地忽略标题的主旨，将这幅漫画称为"1909年定理"，认为摩天楼这种乌托邦装置，可以在单一的基础上创生无限数目的处女地。"建筑内部的'生活'相应地支离：在82层，一只驴子由空洞里抽身而退；在81层，一对都会的男女正向一架飞机挥手致意。" [2] 楼层上的事件是如此断然地互不相干，以至于难以想象它们是同一图景的局部。在这一隐喻传统乡村和现代都市图景的巨大反差的分析中，库哈斯认为：建筑内部的生活和事件是如此的残酷脱节和支离破碎，似乎与建筑是一个整体这一

⑤ 发表在1909年《生活》杂志上的漫画
The cartoon published in *Life* magazine in 1909

事实相矛盾，建筑并非是合乎功能逻辑的空间组合，它完全可以变成个人隐私的堆栈。

70 years after its publication, Walker's cartoon was rediscovered by Rem Koolhaas and extensively analyzed in his seminal book, *Delirious New York*. Koolhaas ignored the thrust of its caption and called it "1909 Theorem", believing that the utopian device of skyscrapers could create an infinite number of virgin sites on a single basis. "The 'life' inside the building is correspondingly fractured: on level 82 a donkey shrinks back from the void, on 81 a cosmopolitan couple hails an airplane."[2] Incidents on the floors are so brutally disjointed that they cannot conceivably be part of the same scenario. In this analysis of the huge contrast between traditional rural and modern urban landscapes, Koolhaas believes that the disconnectedness of the aerial plots seemingly contradicts the fact that, together, they add up to a single building, and that the building is not a functional and logical spatial combination, but can be turned into a stack of individual privacies.

随后，库哈斯还尖锐地讽刺了建筑师的保守和落后，他指出，当专业建筑杂志还在孜孜于"布扎"建筑时，发表在一本大众杂志上的一个漫画家提出的建筑设想，早已超越了正统建筑学的知识想象，民众比曼哈顿的建筑师对摩天楼的潜力更有直觉。实际上在库哈斯之前，勒·柯布西耶也曾讨论过类似的理念，其著名的集合住宅 (Unité d'Habitation) 思想，在一个大的结构支撑框架中，插入一个两层高的预制住宅，不仅预示了预制建筑这一新建筑体系的发展，更是企图通过空间的变革来改变生活（图⑥）。

Later, Koolhaas also sharply satirized the conservatism and backwardness of architects, pointing out that while the architectural magazines of the time were still devoted to Beaux-Arts, the architectural vision of a cartoonist published in a popular magazine had gone beyond the imagination of orthodox architecture and the people had intuited the promise of the Skyscraper more profoundly than Manhattan's architects. In fact, before Koolhaas, Le Corbusier had discussed similar ideas, and his famous concept of Unité d' Habitation suggesting a support frame into which individual prefabricated dwellings might be inserted like bottles into a wine rack, not only prefigured much of what was to follow in prefabricated architecture, but also attempted to change life through the transformation of space (Figure ⑥).

直接受沃克的漫画启发的是 SITE 事务所。在 1980 年代，SITE 发表了"高层住宅"项目的设计方案，一个允许个人自由和表达的住宅的幻想 2）。SITE 通过对漫画轮廓的充实和植物的密集种植，将漫画转变成了更为具体的设计图解，并

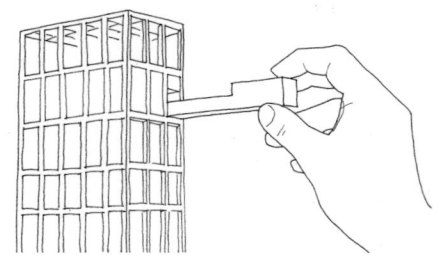

⑥ 勒·柯布西耶集合住宅的框架体系
Framework system of Le Corbusier's United Habitation

预测了绿色摩天大楼在未来的发展趋势（图⑦、⑧）。

The SITE firm was directly inspired by Walker's cartoon. In the 1980s, SITE published the design of "Highrise of Homes" project, a fantasy of highrise housing that would allow individual freedom and expression[2]. SITE's fleshing out of his cartoon's outlines and dense proliferation of its plantings transforms the cartoon into a different kind of art and anticipates a trend found in today's green skyscraper proposals (Figures ⑦ and ⑧).

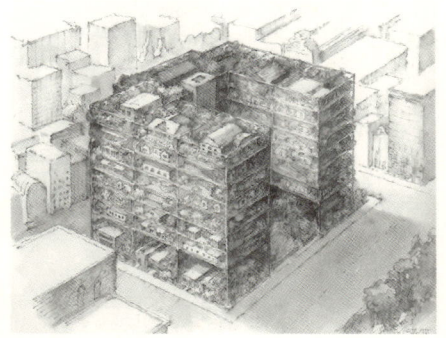

⑦⑧ SITE 建筑事务所关于"高层住宅"的设计方案
Design scheme of "high-rise housing" by SITE Architecture Office

在 2000 年，在德国汉诺威世博会的荷兰馆设计中，MVRDV 进一步发展了 SITE 的绿色生态的设想[3]，显然是 1909 年那幅漫画的绿色生态技术的最新诠释（图⑨）。有趣的是，尽管讨论的都是高层建筑的居住问题，但无论是沃克还是 SITE，最终呈现的都只是局部的或多层的空间图景，而且各个楼层以及其中置入的空间单元都各自独立，正如库哈斯所描述的是一个纯粹私密性的空间堆栈。而 MVRDV 在荷兰馆的设计中用外挂的斜向楼梯将原本各自独立的水平向空间贯通起来，似乎与紫泥堂的改造设计的空间意象更为接近。

In 2000, MVRDV further developed SITE's verdant interpretation[3] in the design of the Dutch Pavilion at Expo Hannover, Germany, which is apparently the latest verdant interpretation of the 1909 cartoon(Figure ⑨). An interesting phenomenon is that although the issue under discussion was living problems of high-risers, what both Walker and SITE finally presented was only a partial or multi-storey spatial picture, and each floor and space unit placed in it were independent, just like the purely private space stack described by Koolhaas. In the design of the Dutch Pavilion, MVRDV uses inclined external staircase to connect the originally independent horizontal floors, which seems to be closer to the space image of the renovation design of the Zi Ni project.

3 加厚的空间边界与潜能分化的空间场域
3 Thickened Space Boundary and Potential Differentiation of Space Field

由于改造设计的空间原型是基于 6 位"斜杠青年"考虑，每一套单元都要基于各自的生活故事，在一个既有的结构框架中展开空间叙事。因此，设计的起点始于一种内部性，并充分体现在历史遗存的静态结构与混杂而不确定的空间使用之间的矛盾。

⑨ 2000 年德国汉诺威世博会的荷兰馆
The Dutch Pavilion for Expo 2000 Hannover, Germany

Because the space prototype of the renovation design is based on six slash youths, each set of units should be based on their own life stories, and space narrative

173

| 屋顶类型
Roof type | 公寓类型
Apartment type | 阳台类型
Balcony type | 入口类型
Entrance type | 卫生间类型
Toilet type | 落地窗类型
French window type | 窗类型
Window type |

⑩ 拆解后的各种建筑构件和空间元素
Disassembled architectural components and spatial elements

should be carried out in the existing structural framework. Therefore, the design begins with a kind of internality as starting point and fully reflects the contradiction between the static structure of historical relics and the mixed and uncertain use of space.

⑪ 西南角改造前后对比
The southwest corner before and after renovation

⑫ 西立面改造前后对比
The west elevation before and after renovation

⑬ 东南角改造前后对比
The southeast corner before and after renovation

建筑师在与既有的梁板柱的纠缠与妥协中，最终所形成的6个空间单元形态各异，材料和色彩混搭，构造组合多元。它们不仅有各自的入户花园甚至是后庭院，每一个起居空间、卧室、卫生间、户内楼梯以及门窗都有独特的形式；数十种不同的建筑构件以及清水红砖墙和波形镀锌板等廉价材料的碎片化组合，不仅使整个空间恍如一个充满了未知性的迷宫，而且还呈现出一种自建的不确定性，极大地模糊了建筑师统一设计的整体感（图⑩～⑲）。令人印象深刻是顶楼最大的以及与其邻接的最小的空间单元。最大一套的原型是一个三口之家，依据日常居住和手工皮具制作的用途，第三层6米高的空间被划分为两层，底层除了入户空间外全部用于工作室和作品陈列，通高的落地窗不仅使室内有着良好的景观视线，也将皮具制作的工艺流程全部展示出来；上层的居住空间是通过半室外平台上的圆形坡道联接，坡道由超过身高的黑色金属薄板围合，当沿着坡道缓步而上时，由于空间相对封闭而致使中间一小段完全没有光照，暗黑的效果会令访客心起疑惑而自然停下脚步，从而巧妙地划分出楼上私密和楼下公共的空间（图⑳、㉑）。

⑭ 改造后厂区鸟瞰图
Bird's eye view of the workshop area after renovation

With hesitation and compromise in the contemplation of the existing beams, slabs and columns, the architects finally designed six space units with different shapes and mixed materials in various colors to construct multiple structural combinations. The units not only have their own gardens and even back courtyards, but also have unique forms for each living room, bedroom, bathroom, indoor stairs, doors and windows. The fragmented combination of dozens of different building components and cheap materials such as clear red brick walls and corrugated galvanized sheets not only makes the whole space like a maze full of unknowns, but also presents a kind of uncertainty of private building, which greatly blurs the associative perception of the architect's unified design (Figures ⑩ ~ ⑲). The largest unit on the top floor and its adjacent unit, the smallest one, are most impressive. The prototype of the largest unit is for a family of three. Taking into account of their daily life and work of leather goods handmaking, the 6m high space of the third floor is divided into two levels. The ground floor except the entrance space is all for studio and work display. The high French window provides good line of sight for not only indoor landscape, but also display of the whole process of leather goods handmaking. The living space on

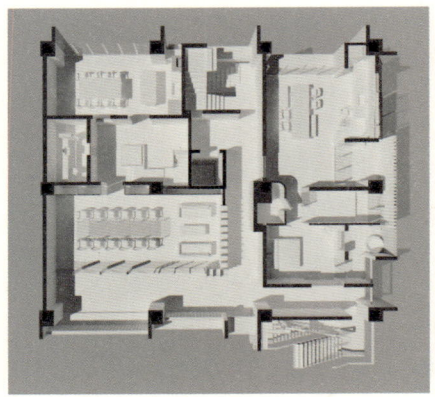

⑮ 二层平面
Plan of the second floor

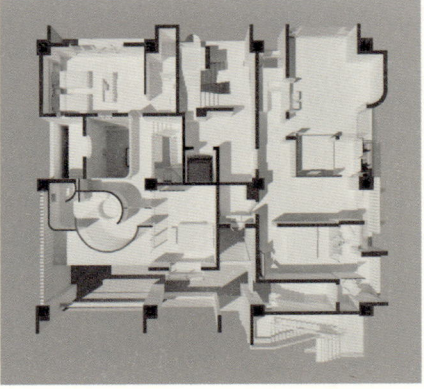

⑯ 二层夹层平面
Plan of the intermediate floor above the second floor

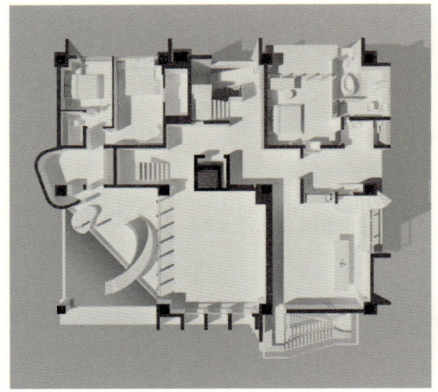

⑰ 三层平面
Plan of the third floor

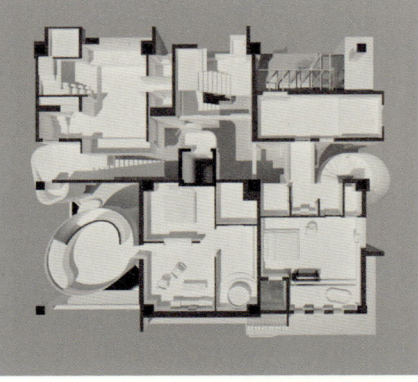

⑱ 三层夹层平面
Plan of the intermediate floor above the third floor

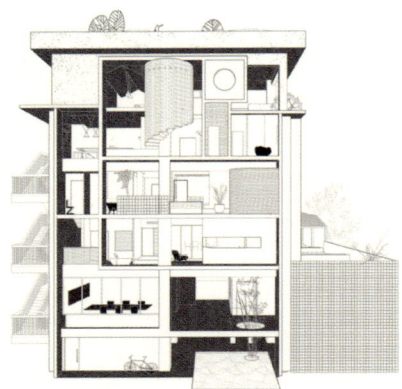

⑲ 立面透视
Perspective view of the elevation

⑳ 坡道下的敞厅
Open hall under the ramp

㉑ 黑色圆形坡道
Black circular ramp

㉒ 混淆室内外界限的坡顶处理
The rump roof blurring interior and exterior boundaries

㉓ 最小单元
The smallest unit

㉔ 取景茶室
Teahouse with a view

the upper level is connected by a circular ramp, which is enclosed by black metal sheet taller than human height, on the semi-outdoor platform. When walking slowly along the ramp, due to the half-closed nature of the space, one would pass a purely dark section in the middle and may feel confused and thus halt naturally. In this way, the private space upstairs and the public space downstairs are cleverly distinguished (Figures ⑳ and ㉑).

最小单元的主人是单身汉设计师，面积仅有 35 平方米，在这一极限状态下，采用复式空间的手法，通过五六级踏步便衔接了从胶囊式卧室、半开敞的卫生间以及开放的工作室这一完整的空间序列。整个单元体块悬挑而出，顶部用波形瓦覆盖，在半开敞的空间中有意造成一种室外的效果。当行走在过道中，仿佛置身于一条狭窄的传统街巷，窗口投射出的光亮会令人流连驻足，欣赏橱窗里展示的工匠师傅的手工制品（图㉒、㉓）。

The owner of the smallest unit is a bachelor designer. With an extremely small area of 35sqm, the approach of duplex space is adopted, and the complete space sequence from capsule bedroom, semi-open bathroom to open studio is connected through merely five or six steps. The entire unit volume is cantilevered and topped with corrugated tiles, intentionally creating an outdoor effect in the semi-open space. When walking in the corridor, one would feel like in a narrow traditional street, and be tempted by the window lights to stop and enjoy the handicrafts displayed in the window (Figures ㉒ and ㉓).

另外，各种复合或混杂的功能空间几乎在每一个空间单元中都有。例如在第二层的夹层空间单元中，针对主人品茶的嗜好，在正对入口的空间设置了一个半通透的和室，它既可开放成为客厅的扩展区，又可独立成茶室，拉上隔板门，晚上就成了卧室。看似很小的客厅可向 4 个方向扩展，形成一人阅读、双人对弈、三人对饮、众人畅谈、可聚可散的自由空间（图㉔）。

In addition, a variety of complex or mixed functional space can be seen in almost every space unit. For example, in the intermediate floor space above the second floor, catering to the owner's tea tasting hobby, a semi-transparent tatami room is set up facing the entrance, which can be opened as an extension of the living room, serve as independent tea room, and even bedroom at night when the partition door is pulled up. The seemingly small living room can be expanded in four directions to form a free space for one person to read, two people to play chess, three people to drink and more people to chit-chat, where people can both get together or scatter around (Figure ㉔).

由于"斜杠青年"去中心化的内在特质，空间等级亟需被打破，因此6套空间单元可以像空间堆栈一样放置在结构空间中的任意位置。另外，不仅每两套单元共享着入户的花园甚至后花园，而且各套单元之间还有意设置了多处公与私空间边界不确定的开放空间。所以身在其间，不仅可以通过大面积的落地窗或横向的长窗看到各位艺术家创作或手工制作的过程，也可通过自家的窗户和小阳台楼上楼下地聊天打招呼，屋顶开放的平台又为更多的家庭成员或访客提供了一处大聚会的场所。这种空间社会关联度的反复强化，使得整个建筑就像一个垂直的迷你社区（图㉕）。

㉕ 创建邻里关系的立面
The facade that creates neighborhood relationship

Because of the inherent characteristics of decentralization of "slash youth", the spatial hierarchy needs to be broken, so the six spatial units can be placed in any position in the structural space like spatial stacks. Moreover, an entrance garden or even back garden is shared by every two units, and a number of open spaces with uncertain boundaries between public and private spaces are also intentionally set up. Therefore, people living here can not only see artists' creation or hand-making process through the large French windows or horizontal long windows, but also chat and greet neighbors through their own windows and small balconies upstairs or downstairs. The open platform on the roof provides a place for more family members or visitors to gather. The repeated strengthening of spatial social relevance turns the whole building into a vertical mini-community (Figure ㉕).

如果紫泥堂的改造设计沿用沃克或SITE的空间策略的话，那么建筑最终呈现的空间意象即会与沃克和SITE的极为相似，即在一个完整的空间结构之中，于各层上塞入风格独特以至碎片化的居住单元。为了平衡空间的整一化与碎片化的矛盾，在保留原有建筑厚重的檐口、拆除外围护墙体的基础上，从建筑的外边柱上出挑了一系列宽大的板状构件，致使整个建筑表皮有了一个空间厚度。向内，这一加厚的界面与6个空间单元之间留有一定的间隙，不仅有效地化约了每层6米通高的空间尺度，而且还创造出了邻里之间相互交流的冗余空间（图㉖）；向外，这一加厚界面灰白的色彩与建筑檐口原有混凝土的颜色有着明显的区分，不仅凸显出新旧建筑的时间上的差异，而且整个板状构件就像一个巨型博古架，将内部空间多样化的几何形体、材料构件，以及所发生的生活和事件，向外展示了出来，每当夜幕降临，整个建筑仿佛一系列带框的巨幕，播放着一场场生动的日常生活电影（图㉗、㉘）。

178

㉖ 加厚边界与建筑之间的冗余空间
Thickened boundary and surplus space between buildings

㉗ 夜幕下的建筑立面
Building facade after nightfall

㉘ 改造后的围墙与入口
Modified wall and entrance

If the renovation design of Zi Ni project follows the space strategy of Walker or SITE, the final space image of the building would be very similar to that of Walker and SITE, i.e., stacking unique and even fragmented living units into each floor in a complete space structure. In order to balance the contradiction between the integration and fragmentation of space, on the basis of retaining the thick eaves of the original building and removing the peripheral wall, a series of broad plate-shaped components are cantilevered from the outer columns of the building, resulting in a "space thickness" of the whole building skin. Internally, a certain gap is preserved between the thickened interface and the 6 space units, which not only effectively reduces the space scale of each 6m high floor, but also creates surplus space for communication between neighbors (Figure ㉖). Externally, the gray color of this thickened interface is clearly distinguished from the original concrete color of the cornice of the building, which not only highlights the age difference between the old and new buildings, but also makes the whole plate-like component like a giant curio shelf, which shows the diversified geometric shapes and material components of the internal space, as well as the life and events taking place in the building. After every nightfall, the whole building looks like a series of framed giant screens, on which vivid movies of daily life are broadcasted live (Figures ㉗ and ㉘).

这种加厚的策略还延续到了室外的空间设计上。在保留了原建筑入口处一堵废弃墙体的基础上，通过新置入的几何形体与场地原有榕树的组合，提供了一处室外的喝茶小憩的场所，这一进入建筑的前奏空间，仿佛从主体建筑中溢出，进一步凸显出室内外空间的无界感。这种空间场域无界感的反复出现，不仅使得空间的复合使用得以可能，创造了私人空间和公共空间相互渗透的弹性界域，也进一步表征出"斜杠青年"职业身份的潜能分化（图㉙、㉚）。

This strategy of thickening is further applied to outdoor space design. On the basis of retaining an abandoned wall at the entrance of the original building and through combining the new geometric shape and the original banyan tree, an outdoor place for tea and leisure is created, which seems to be overflowing from the main building and further highlights the borderless trait of indoor and outdoor space. The repeated appearance of the borderless trait of space field not only makes the multiple use of space possible and creates an elastic boundary for mutual penetration of private and public spaces, but also further characterizes the potential differentiation of the professional identity of "slash youth" (Figures ㉙ and ㉚).

当置身于整个紫泥糖厂的背景中，改造后的建筑则更像是一个大社区的公共客厅，在这一竖向空间中，设计不仅试图解决私人日常和公共生活的融合，成为一个有内聚力的空间容器，而且还试图将建筑内向的丰富活动与厂区的街道空间相结合。这一内联和外呈的空间策略，在将"斜杠青年"的工作和生活展示的同时，也将工遗景观和自然景观联结成了一个互为图底的展示整体。

Against the background of the whole Zi Ni Sugar Factory, the renovated building is more like a public parlor of a large community. In this vertical space, the design attempts not only to integrate private daily life and public life to create a cohesive space container, but also to combine the rich activities inside the building with the street space of the factory area. This spatial strategy of internal connection and external presentation not only displays the work and life of "slash youth", but also links the landscape of industrial heritage and natural landscape, with their swappable roles of principal and background, as a whole for display.

4 结语：互联网时代的"社会冷凝器"[4]
4 Conclusion: Social Condenser in the Internet Age [4]

如果将这个改造设计看作是一次空间实验，即会使人联想起1920年代苏联一批先锋艺术家和建筑师关于"社会冷凝器"的研究。在前苏联的社会政治背景下，他们试图提出一种全新的建筑类型来创造一种新的人类集体——共同居住、共同生产、共同进行智力和体力劳动，是一种具有理性和激情、情感和美学的集体。尽管"社会冷凝器"还包括了各项社会的、经济的和物质的基础设施，是一个日常生活的平凡琐事以及超验和幻想的不羁领域，但颇具启发的是，"社会冷凝器"探讨的是整合居住、工作和公共空间的一种全新的建筑类型。在这个意义上，不妨将紫泥堂的改造看作是"社会冷凝器"思想的回归，这一空间实验可以使我们超越特定的历史和地点美学，重启关于互联网时代居住空间可能性的思考。

If this renovation design is regarded as a space experiment, it would remind people of the research on "social condenser" by a group of avant-garde artists and architects in the Soviet Union in the 1920s. Against the social and political backdrop of the former Soviet Union, they tried to put forward a new type of architecture to create a brand-new human collective featuring co-living, co-production and co-laboring both physically and intellectually, which is a collective integrating reason and passion, emotion and aesthetics. Although the "social condenser" encompasses social, economic

㉙ 围墙改造后的可活动空间
Movable space after wall modification

and physical infrastructures, and is about trivial and ordinary everyday life as well as the unruly realm of transcendence and fantasy, it is quite inspiring that it also explores a new type of architecture that integrates living, working and public space. In this sense, the Zi Ni renovation project can be regarded as a return to the idea of "social condenser", a space experiment that enables us to transcend the aesthetics of specific history and place, and to restimulate our thinking about the possibilities of living space in the Internet era.

当然，这样的空间试验如果不进一步锚定于既定的社会和城市脉络中，并开始重新定义与激活，使其成为建筑思想和实践的载体，便会丧失"社会冷凝器"所具有的多元分化的潜能，也必然会成为资本逻辑下的空间矫情。

Of course, if such a space experiment is not further anchored in the established social and urban context, and begins to redefine and activate the space, making it the vehicle of architectural ideas and practices, it will lose the potential of pluralistic differentiation of "social condenser", and will inevitably become "space affectation" manipulated by the logic of capital.

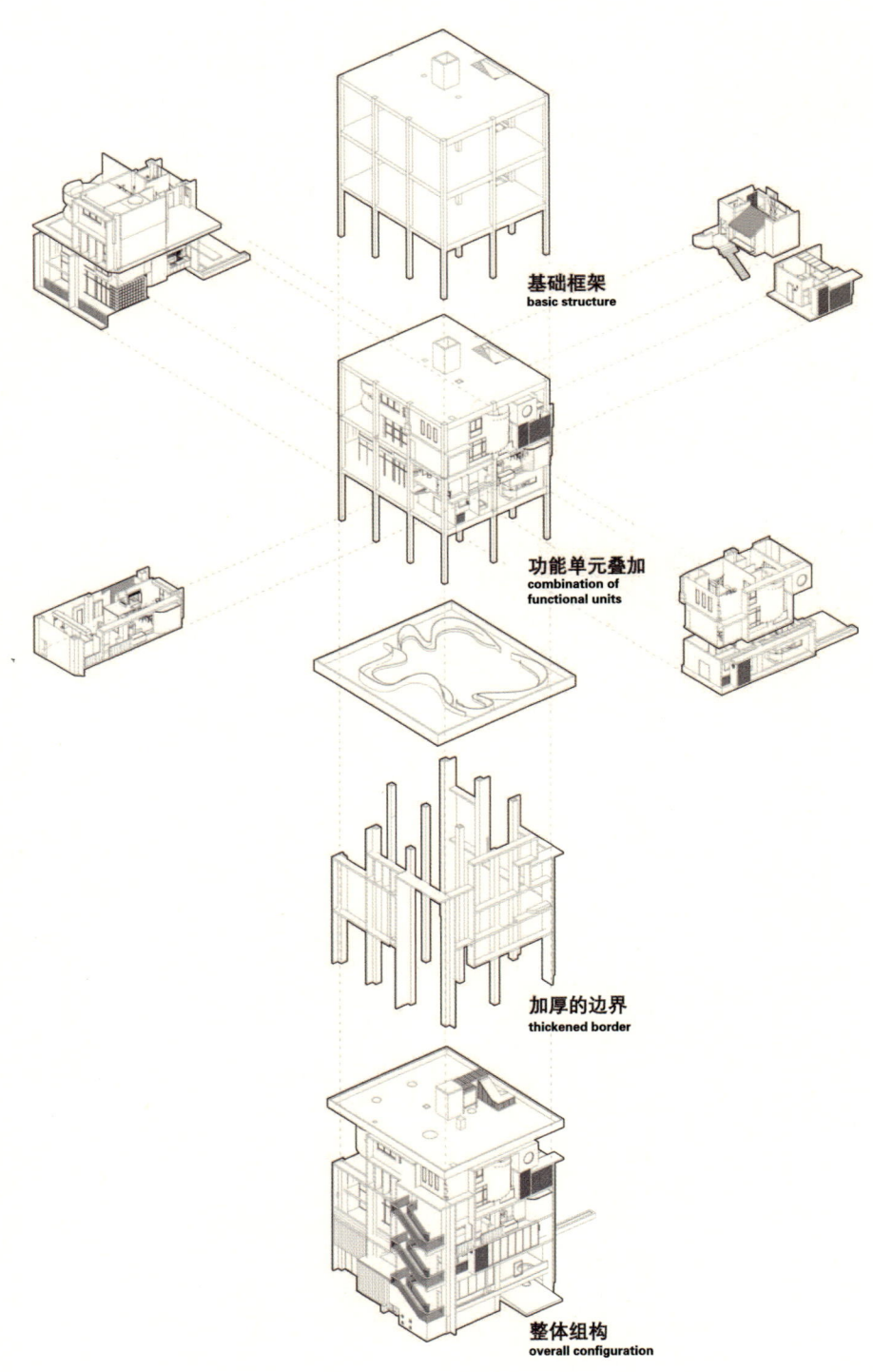

㉚ 加厚边界与建筑其他要素的空间关系
Spatial relationship between the thickened border and other elements of the building

注释 Notes

1) 斜杠青年来源于英文 slash，出自《纽约时报》专栏作家麦瑞克·阿尔伯撰写的书籍《双重职业》，指的是一群不再满足"专一职业"的生活方式，而选择拥有多重职业和身份的多元生活的人群。
The term "slash youth" originates from the book *Dual Career* written by *New York Times* columnist Merrick Alber. It refers to a group of people who are no longer satisfied with the single career lifestyle, but choose to live a pluralistic life with multiple careers and identities.

2) SITE 认为沃克 1909 年的漫画的形象显然是关键的灵感和典范。
SITE believes that Walker's 1909 cartoon image is clearly a key inspiration and exemplar.

3) MVRDV 可能受到了库哈斯影响，因为 MVRDV 事务所的两名负责人曾为 OMA 工作过。
MVRDV may have been influenced by Koolhaas because two of the principals of MVRDV had worked for OMA.

4) "社会冷凝器"是 1928 年苏联的建筑师莫伊谢伊·金兹伯格 (Moisei Ginzburg) 在第一届 OSA 会议中提出的混杂了多种功能和公共空间的一种建筑类型。
The "social condenser" is a type of architecture proposed by architect Moisei Ginzburg of Soviet Union in the first OSA conference in 1928, which mixes multiple functions and public spaces.

参考文献 References

[1] ArchiTakes. Influential "Life" Cartoon Turns 100 [EB/OL]. [2009-08-05]. http://www.architakes.com/?p=1687.

[2] 雷姆·库哈斯. 癫狂的纽约 [M]. 唐克杨，译. 北京：生活·读书·新知三联书店，2015:129.
Rem Koolhaas. Crazy New York[M]. Tang Keyang, translator. Beijing: SDX Joint Publishing Company, 2015:129.

图片来源 Image source

① 油印紫泥糖厂志
Figure ①: Mimeograph of Zi Ni Sugar Factory

⑤ 雷姆·库哈斯《疯狂的纽约》，2015:128
Figure ⑤: Rem Koolhaas. *Crazy New York*. 2015: 128

⑥，⑨ http://www.architakes.com/?p=1687.

⑦~⑧ https://cn.bing.com/images/

⑪~⑳，㉓~㉕，㉗，㉙，㉚ 由扉美术馆提供
Figures ⑪~⑳，㉓~㉕，㉗，㉙，㉚ provided by FEI Arts

其余图片均为本文作者拍摄、绘制
The rest of the pictures are taken and drawn by the author of this article

学术评论二
Academic Reviews 2

"走向策展"和"公众主体"的空间生产
The Production of Space "Moving Towards Curation" and "with Public as Subject"

辛塞波
Xin Saibo

同济大学哲学系博士后
Postdoctoral Fellow,
Department of Philosophy,
Tongji University

本文是刊发于《公共艺术》3/2021 文章的调整版本。
This article is a revised version of the one published in *Public Art*, 3/2021.

摘 要

"菜市场美术馆"带给人们的思考不是它到底该不该获奖,而是要用我们每个人自己的理性去思考:人类世里到底需要怎样的建筑?公众到底有没有权利去居有城市空间?笔者以为,由何志森"改造"的"菜市场美术馆"是基于日常生活现象的批判性作品,它与通常理解的建筑设计不同,不涉及历史传承、审美审丑的问题,也与城市的精细治理、机制平衡无关。它也不是某个人或某群人的研究专题,而是每个人的事情,人人都从空间出发做出自己的作品,最后形成总体的艺术作品。从这个意义上说,"菜市场美术馆"构造了一个真正意义上的正义社会、人文城市的基本模型和终极目标。

Abstract

The thinking that the "Market Museum" stimulated is not whether it should be awarded, but the following issues that we should ponder by our own rationality: What kind of architecture is needed in the Anthropocene? Do the public have the right to inhabit urban space? I believe that the "Market Museum" "transformed" by Jason Zhisen Ho is a critical work based on the phenomenon of daily life. It is different from the commonly understood architectural design, which does not involve the topic of historical inheritance, aesthetics and anti-aesthetics, and has nothing to do with micro governance and institutional balance of the city. It is not the research topic of a certain person or a group of people but something that engages everyone. Everyone can make his own work from space, and finally forms an overall work of art. In this sense, "Market Museum" constructs the basic model and realizes the ultimate goal of a truly just society and humane city.

关键词

菜市场美术馆;对城市的权利;走向策展;公众主体;艺术作品

Keywords

market museum; right to the city; moving towards curation; with public as subject; works of art

由建筑师何志森"改造"的"菜市场美术馆"（图①）入选由《三联生活周刊》主办的首届人文建筑/城市评奖提名，但没有获奖，让人感到有些遗憾。何志森在某社交媒体上说："虽然没获奖，但还是很开心，至少他们被'看到'了。谢谢过去4年来所有关注和支持菜市场项目的人。菜市场的物理空间已永远消失，但联结还在延续。……希望有一天，中国有更多的作品能够摆脱建造的局限，重新书写'建筑'的定义。"笔者以为，"菜市场美术馆"虽然没有获奖，但它构造了一个真正意义上的正义社会、人文城市的基本模型和终极目标。

① 农林菜市场外观
The appearance of Nonglin Market

The Market Museum (Figure ①) "transformed" by architect Jason Zhisen Ho, was nominated for the first City for Humanity Awards sponsored by *Sanlian Lifeweek Magazine*, but missed it—which is somewhat a pity. Jason commented on a social media: "Although we didn't win the award, we are very happy for at least they were seen. We are so grateful to all the people who have followed and supported the market project over the past 4 years. Though the physical space of the market has disappeared forever, the connections it built are still extending… I hope that one day, more works in China will be able to go beyond the limitations of construction and rewrite the definition of 'architecture'." In my view, although the Market Museum missed the award, it has constructed the basic model and realized the ultimate goal of a truly just society and humane city.

1 "菜市场美术馆"的特别之处
1 Special Features of "Market Museum"

在三联人文城市奖之社区营造奖的提名作品"菜市场美术馆"的评审意见中，关键词有"微设计""改造""当代设计""介入""提升""跨界"，这样的关键词所指涉的是以建筑师和艺术家为主体的为城市提升改造所做的专业设计，不过是设计的方式发生了一些变化，比如说向普通百姓的日常生活权益的倾斜。但笔者以为，"菜市场美术馆"与其他作品有着本质的区别，它有两个重要特点不容忽视：一个是建筑师作为"不造物"的策展人；还有一个是美术馆的创作主体不是建筑师或者艺术家而是公众。需要指出的是，策展人与公众紧密相连：作为建筑师的策展人将他们盖房子的技术手段放在一边，以自己的示范性行动帮助公众寻找和建立各自的方法，并去实践自己的建筑行动，以使公众创造和自己生存、生活有关的艺术作品。

In the evaluation opinions of the nominated work Market Museum for Community Empowerment of Sanlian City for Humanity Awards, the key words are "micro-design" "transformation" "contemporary design" "intervention" "promotion" and "cross-border". Such keywords refer to the professional design for urban upgrading and transformation with architects and artists as the subject, but some changes have taken place in the way of design, such as the inclination to the rights and interests of ordinary people in daily life. However, I believe that Market Museum is essentially different from other works, and it has two important characteristics that should not be ignored: Firstly, architects are curators who "do not create things". Secondly, the subject of art museum creation is not architects or artists but the public. However, it should be pointed out that the curator and the public are closely linked. The curator, who is also an architect, now puts aside his technical means of building houses but, with his own exemplary actions, helps the public to find and establish their own methods. Moreover, in this case, he can practice his own architectural actions, so as to enable the public to create works of art related to their own livelihood and life.

（1）什么是"不造物"呢？就是说"菜市场美术馆"没有涉及建筑学的核心问题：对材料的物质性操作，而是以"不造物"的方式构建一个"情境"。"菜市场美术馆"形成的与日常生活场境相关的微观氛围，通过具有创造性的"策展"让麻木、无趣甚至利益受到侵犯的生活重新获得一种激情转变，这也就实现了在微观生活细节层面上的情境建构。从这个意义上说，"菜市场美术馆"将"令人动情的情境"当作主题，在日常生活功能上解构了商品交易结构、塑形了全新美好生活的艺术氛围和心理构境。

Firstly, what does "do not create things" mean? In fact, the Market Museum does not deal with the core issue of architecture, i.e., the material operation of materials, but constructs a situation in a way that "does not create things". Through creative "curation", the Market Museum generates a micro-atmosphere relevant to daily life scenes to bring passionate changes to the numb, boring life of underprivileged people, thus realizes the situation construction at the level of micro-life in details. In this sense, themed on "emotional situation", the Market Museum deconstructs the commodity trading structure in daily life function, and shapes the artistic atmosphere and psychological structure of a new and better life.

从建筑学的角度说，何志森确实没干什么，只是做了一个融合氛围的策展工作。"建筑师除了盖房子还能做什么？"也是何志森一直在思考的问题。在对"菜市场美术馆"改造的过程中，何志森将关注的重点放在菜市场和美术馆之间的边界上:"边界两边的气质、情感、思想、文化和价值观不断进行互动、碰撞,甚至是转换,相互尊重却又彼此影响和加持,艺术和生活开始融合,一种新的关系在摊贩与艺术家之间、摊贩与美术馆工作人员之间悄然形成,农林菜市场成为了新的美术馆,摊贩变成了艺术家,而我和扉美术馆所扮演的角色却在慢慢弱化。"[1](图②)

② 菜市场与美术馆的边界
The border between the market and the art museum

From the view of architecture, Jason Zhisen Ho really did nothing but curatorial work of creating harmonious atmosphere. What can architects do besides building houses? This is an issue that Jason has been thinking about. In the process of transforming the Market Museum, he focused on the border between the market and the art museum: "The temperament, emotion, thought, culture and values on the two sides of the border have been constantly interacting and colliding with and even transforming while respecting, influencing and supporting each other. In the meanwhile, art and life began to merge, a new relationship has been quietly formed between vendors and artists, vendors and art museum staff. The Nonglin Market has emerged as a new art museum, while the roles of me and FEI Arts are fading slowly."[1] (Figure ②)

需要强调的是,这里说的策展和我们将建筑模型和艺术作品放在美术馆里进行展示的那种完全不同,它是由建筑师进行组织、策划的,具有强大示范效应的一种空间性运动,它的目的是为生活在都市里的居民争取对空间的权利。这样,公众可以在他们的作品或者项目中进行空间再生产。这里,策展人把公众对于城市空间的权利放在首要位置,从社会关系的角度来组织和示范各种空间的可能性,这就使建筑师的工作大部分变成了对空间的策展,以改造现有的社会空间关系。笔者以为,"走向策展",是释放何志森作为建筑师的乌托邦理想的最好途径。

What needs to be emphasized is that the curation here is entirely different from its normal definition, i.e., staging an exhibition of architectural models and works of art in art museums. It is a spatial movement organized and planned by architects, which has a strong demonstration effect. Its purpose is to strive for the right to urban space for the residents living in the city. In this way, the public can reproduce space in their works or projects. Here, the curator put the public's right to urban space in the first place, organizing and demonstrating the possibilities of various spaces from the perspective of social relations. Therefore, most of the architect's work is to "curate"—arranging the space to transform the existing social space relations. In my opinion, "moving towards curation" is the best way to realize Jason Zhisen Ho's Utopian ideal as an architect.

列斐伏尔的《空间的生产》告诉我们，当推动空间生产的动力和内在机制不是社会关系的矛盾与社会实践，而是抽象的资本循环与价值增值规律时，空间生产就会转变成物质产品的生产，空间不是社会关系的产物而被还原为产品的生产场地。我们经常去的菜市场大概属于此类，就是辖区居民和市场摊贩的一个商品买卖关系发生的场所。而"菜市场美术馆"颠覆了我们对菜市场的认识，它超越了空间被分割、分隔的狭隘，不仅具有批判性反思当下社会内在矛盾的意义，而且包含通过"策展"而达到未来创造新文明可能性的诗性意义。

Lefebvre's *The Production of Space* tells us that when the driving force and internal mechanism of space production are not the conficts and social practice of social relations, but the abstract laws of capital circulation and value appreciation, space production will be transformed into the production of material products, and space will not be the product of social relations but be reduced to the production site of products. The wet market we often go to probably belongs to this category, which is a place where the trading relationship between local residents and market vendors takes place. However, the Market Museum subverts our understanding of wet markets. Transcending the narrow division of space, it not only has the significance of critical reflection on the internal contradictions of the current society, but also contains the poetic significance of the possibility of creating a new civilization in the future through "curation".

（2）"公众作为主体"如何理解呢？这与建筑师作为主体是相对而言的，"菜市场美术馆"改造的主角并非建筑师，而是这个菜市场的摊贩，这是何志森特别强调的。改造后的菜市场几乎看不到建筑师留下的专业痕迹，体现得更多的是菜市场中的人们通过对特定时空的理解来打开他们日常生活的努力。何志森曾说："在我建议学生拍下摊贩们双手的照片后，摊贩把他们双手的照片领了回去，自发在菜市场布展。让我没有意料到的是，他们把自己双手的照片放在了政府颁发的营业执照的旁边，形成了一个鲜明的对比。在之后的时间里，双手的照片神奇地变成了一个摊贩与摊贩之间、摊贩与当地居民之间相互联结的媒介。"

Secondly, how to understand "public as the subject"? This is relative to "architect as the subject". The protagonist of the transformation of Market Museum is not the architect, but the vendors of the market, which is particularly emphasized by Jason Zhisen Ho. After transformation, there is almost no professional traces left by architects in the market, but reflects more the efforts of people in the market to open up their daily life through their understanding of specific time and space.

Jason Zhisen Ho once said: "After the students had taken photos of the vendors' hands as suggested by me, the vendors claimed their photos and voluntarily displayed them in the market. What I didn't expect was that they put the picture of their hands next to the business license issued by the authority, which formed a sharp contrast. Later on, the photos magically became a communication medium between vendors and vendors, as well as vendors and local residents."

在菜市场改造中，何志森尊重摊贩们内心深处的愿望，希望他们的努力可以被别人看到，希望他们的世界不会被专业的改造活动所摧毁。何志森选择"个人叙事"作为美术馆改造的基础，是出于对每个人都可能遭受不公对待的普遍承认和抵抗，他要让菜市场中的每个摊贩都有讲自己故事的机会。需要指出的是，菜市场的摊贩并非就是一个共同体，在它内部，比起消除差异、建立共识的构想，一个建立在公众基础之上的"异识"细分更加令人期待。[1] 当然，这绝非一项解决冲突的事务，而是一种将公众作为主体的关乎自由、法则和公正的希望之举。

In the transformation of the market, Jason Zhisen Ho respects the deep wishes of the vendors in the hope that their efforts can be seen by others and their world will not be destroyed by professional transformation activities. Jason chose "personal narrative" as the basis of the transformation of the art museum, out of the universal recognition and resistance to the unfair treatment that everyone may suffer, and he wanted every vendor in the market to have the opportunity to tell his/her own story. It needs to be pointed out that the market vendors are not a unity. For the vendors, compared with eliminating differences and establishing consensus, respecting "differences" based on the public is more worth expecting.[1] Of course, this is not a matter of conflict resolution, but a matter of hope for freedom, law and justice, with the public as the subject.

然而，仅从个人的权利受到威胁与侵犯的角度去思考空间就可以了吗？显然也不是。这里的重点是要使空间走向个人作品，也就是要打开每一个人的日常生活，使"我"的时空成为艺术作品，使"我"的作为作品的生活方式成为城市的一部分，这才是"公众作为主体"的真正含义。（图③）

However, is it proper to think about space only in terms of threats and violations of individual rights? Obviously not. The key point here is to make space move towards personal works, i.e., to open up everyone's daily life, to turn "my" time and space into work of art, and to turn "my" way of life into work of art that are part of the city. This is what "public as subject" truly means. (Figure ③)

摊贩们逐渐发现，被打开的每一个人的日常生活都有可能成为艺术作品。这里所指的艺术作品的创造不是艺术品的创造，而是指摊贩们自觉的行为，自我再生产自己的条件，适应这些条件并实现身体、欲望、时间、空间，并使之成为自我创造物。[2] 而要走向人人的建筑行动，就是让每个人都讲出自己的建筑故事，还给每个人讲述自己的居住和行动空间的权利。作为公众，不是要去作品中找那个建筑师刻意设计并巧妙地告诉他们的东西，而是要用别人的建筑来实践自己的建筑，将建筑师设计的建筑空间变成自己居有的建筑空间。

The vendors gradually find that the daily life of everyone, once opened up, may become a work of art. The creation of works of art here doesn't mean to create artworks, but refers to the conscious behavior of the vendors, the conditions of their self-reproduction, as well as their adaptation to these conditions and realization of body, desire, time and space to make it a self-creation.[2] To move towards everyone's architectural action is to let everyone tell their own architectural stories, and to give everyone the right to tell about their own life and action space. The public are not supposed to look for what the architect deliberately designed and skillfully tell them in the works, but to use other people's architecture to practice their own architecture,

③ 菜市场摊主把他们和工作坊学生，还有和何志森的合照悬挂在档口上
The vendors hung their pictures with the workshop students and Jason Zhisen Ho on their stalls

and to turn the architectural space designed by the architect into their own architectural space.

（3）对于"菜市场美术馆"存在的意义，何志森说："在和相关部门沟通的时候，他们告诉我菜市场拆除之后会变成一个公园，造福社区的居民——公园不就是一个联结人与人的场所吗？公园当然是。但和菜市场不一样的是：公园提供的更多是以休闲、娱乐、社交为目的的日常活动，它只考虑了一部分人，或者说某一人群，主要为中产阶层的需求。"从生产力与生产关系的角度说，"以休闲、娱乐、社交为目的的日常活动"的公园，实际上是由于劳作时间的缩短而创造的更多时间和空间的载体，它是德波说的"革命性游戏"与资产阶级争夺闲暇时间和生活空间的重要工具。

Thirdly, regarding for the significance of the existence of Market Museum, Jason said: "When we communicated with relevant government departments, we were told that after the demolition of the market, it would be turned into a park to benefit the residents of the community—isn't the park a place to connect people, they said. Of course, a park can connect people. But unlike the market, the park mainly offers daily activities for leisure, entertainment and socializing purposes, and only concerns the needs of part of the people, or a certain group of people, mainly the middle class." From the perspective of productivity and production relations, the park for "daily activities targeting at leisure, entertainment and socializing" is actually the carrier of extra time and space resulted from the shortening of working time. It is an important tool for Debord's "revolutionary game" to compete with the bourgeoisie for leisure time and living space.

对何志森来说，"菜市场美术馆"就是一次"革命性游戏"，它面临一个从内里重新塑形时空的争夺战。从这个意义上说，"菜市场美术馆"打破了由物性建筑和功能区域场境支配的结构，以及这种物性结构在日常生活场境中塑形的空间和心理构境。在主体自身的情境建构实践活动中，"菜市场美术馆"通过艺术手段进行了具有革命性的空间改造，这实际上也是列斐伏尔的空间再生产理论思想的体现。

For Jason Zhisen Ho, the Market Museum is such a "revolutionary game", which faces a battle to reshape time and space from within. In this sense, Market Museum breaks the structure dominated by physical architecture and context of functional area, as well as the spatial and psychological structures shaped by this physical structure in the context of daily life. In the practice of the subject's own situational construction, Market Museum has carried out a revolutionary spatial transformation through artistic means, which is actually an embodiment of Lefebvre's theory of production of space.

列斐伏尔提出空间生产的目的在于真实地改变异化了的生活,以具体的艺术实践直接介入其中。笔者以为,"菜市场美术馆"就是这种超越性的艺术实践,事实证明它并非一个遥不可及的理想,而是有可能在城市的日常生活中实现的。在德波看来,"占领"就是对异化劳动的拒绝,"节日""游戏"是人和时间的真实在场,这也是对所有权威化、专业性的拒绝和批判。这里,对特定空间的利用是为一种使用者的"越轨"。在这种"越轨"中,感知和治理、日常与节庆、社会与脑力之间的分裂被克服,而这一空间揭示了何处是脆弱的领域与可能实现的突破点。通过对爱欲、节庆、游戏、艺术等价值的表达,可以还原生命本体在空间生产中的作用和意义。在空间生产中,它们呈现为身体、欲望、差异、日常生活的再现空间。

Henri Lefebvre argues that the production of space aims to truly change the alienated life, and directly intervene via concrete artistic practices. In my opinion, Market Museum is such a transcendent artistic practice, which proves that it is not an unreachable ideal, but can be realized in the city's daily life. In Debord's view, "occupation" is the rejection of alienated labor; "festival" and "game" are the real presence of people and time, which is also the rejection and criticism of all authoritarianism and professionalism. Here, the use of a particular space is regarded as a "transgression" by users. In such "transgression", the split between perception and governance, daily life and festival, society and intellectual labor is overcome, and such space reveals where the fragile areas and possible breakthrough points are. Through the expression of love, festivals, games, art and other values, we can restore the role and significance of life itself in space production. In the production of space, they appear as the reproduction space of body, desire, differences and daily life.

2 从"设计"走向"策展"
2 From "Design" to "Curation"

如果我们按照今天对建筑师职业的理解,那么人们的生活就会被规划、被设计,日常生活就永远是被异化的。如果想从中逃离出来,我们必须从"设计"走向"策展"。实际上,作为专业人员来说,能够迈出这步绝非易事,这需要极大的勇气、智慧和能力。建筑师如何通过建筑的方式回应今天社会的矛盾和问题？何志森一直在持续思考一种"看不见的建造"，也即是一种对社会关系的建构。实际上，这种社会关系的建构即是空间生产视角下的一种"策展"行动。虽然构建并实践替代性方案很是不易，但何志森的态度和信念是乐观的：只有直面现存方案和替代性方案，以及现有探寻和替代性探寻间碰撞的现实，我们才可构筑能够超越现实并摆脱支配的方案。

Complying with the current interpretation of architects as professionals, people's life will be planned and designed, and daily life will always be alienated. If we want to escape from it, we must move from "design" to "curation". In fact, as a professional, it is not easy to take this step, which requires great courage, wisdom and ability. How do architects respond to the conflicts and problems of today's society through architecture? Jason Zhisen Ho has been thinking about an "invisible construction", that is, a construction of social relations. In fact, the construction of social relation is a kind of "curation" action from the perspective of space production. Although it is not easy to construct and practice alternative solution, Jason's attitude and belief are optimistic: only by facing the reality of the collision between existing solutions and alternative solutions, as well as existing exploration and alternative exploration, can we construct solutions that can transcend reality and get rid of domination.

三联人文城市奖的提名人在谈到提名作品时说："几十平米就能支撑一种新的城市使用方式，就不需要几千几万平米。我们今天还需要推广花很多钱盖大公建的模式吗？城市还需要那么多建筑吗？"[2] 笔者以为，这是一种"增量"转"存量"的政策性说法，如果进一步反思，则是：几十平方米的建筑就值得推广吗？这并非一个面积大小的问题。人类世（Anthropocene）[3] 里到底该做怎样的建筑？在一个标志着人类干预与人类超越的时期，建筑的地位是如何变化的呢？人类世的压力是否会使建筑在未来以一种创造性的姿态造就奇迹呢？笔者以为，还在服务甲方的建筑师，哪怕从事再小的项目，也不过是做了工程师的工作。如果想要真正提高行业的门槛，或者获得让人尊敬的地位，今天的建筑师就需要被重新定位——从"设计"走向"策展"。

"If several tens of square meters can support a new way of using the city, then we don't need tens of thousands of square meters. Do we still need to promote the model of large public buildings that cost a lot of money today? Does the city still need so many buildings?"[2] said one of the nominators of the Sanlian City for

Humanity Awards when talking about the nominated works. In my view, this is a policy-related saying of turning "incremental" to "stock". As we further reflect upon this: "Are buildings of several tens of square meters worth promoting?", we would realize it is not a question of size. What kind of architecture should be built in Anthropocene[3)]? How does the status of architecture change in a period that marks human intervention and human transcendence? Will the pressures of Anthropocene enable architecture to achieve miracles in a creative manner in the future? In my view, when architects are still serving "Party A", even if they are engaged in small projects, they are just doing the work of engineers. In order to really raise the threshold of the industry and to earn respectable status for the professionals, today's architects need to be repositioned—moving from "design" to "curation".

需要强调的是，在"菜市场美术馆"参赛的评审意见中，评委使用了"当代艺术"一词。"当代艺术"所体现的是艺术家对今天社会生活的感受的当代性，艺术家置身的是今天的文化环境，面对的是今天的现实，他们的作品就必然反映今天的时代特征。实际上，今天的建筑已经不能跟着当代艺术走了，也更不能跟着现代艺术走，现代建筑跟着现代艺术走让具象空间变成了抽象空间，形成了今天城市紧张的空间关系，跟着当代艺术走那又怎么样呢？像当代艺术一样关照现实？显然，今天的建筑需要走在当代艺术的前面，需要进行比当代艺术更当代的实践，"策展"不仅是对今天社会现实的表达和反映，也是一种具有未来性的关于社会关系的思考，它需要超越对"物"的展示，走向对"事件"的发动。从这个角度说，策展需要引领当代艺术，在这方面，建筑是否更具示范性呢？[3]193

It should be pointed out that the term "contemporary art" rather than "modern art" is used by the judging panel of the Award in the evaluation opinions of the Market Museum. "Contemporary art" reflects the contemporary nature of the feelings of artists about today's social life for they live in today's cultural environment and face today's reality, so their works will inevitably reflect the characteristics of contemporary times. In fact, today's architecture can no longer follow modern art. As modern architecture follows modern art, concrete space becomes abstract space and has resulted in tense urban spatial relationship now. So what if architecture follows contemporary art? Concern and care about reality like contemporary art? Obviously, today's architecture needs to get ahead of modern art, and carry out practice that is more modern than modern art. "Curation" is also an expression and reflection of today's social reality. Furthermore, it could be a futuristic thinking about social relations, which needs to go beyond the display of "things" to the launch of "events". From this point of view, curation even needs to lead contemporary art. In this respect, isn't architecture more exemplary?[3]193

④ 从美术馆望向菜市场
Looking from the Museum to the market

建筑师从"设计"走向"策展"使空间结果虚拟化，让一个策展事件变成一个美好的乌托邦，这就是建筑师要给出的示范。这要求建筑师要将服从几何和美学要求的设计空间策展成社会空间，使之进入社会空间的生产过程。需要指出的是，作为密切关联空间实践的学科，建筑和城规理所当然地应对空间的生产问题作出回应，但这些探索应是以摆脱旧的学科范式为前提的。列斐伏尔《空间的生产》的总体视角可以促使城市规划、建筑设计的学科专业人士跳出狭隘的专业范畴，将自己的思考和实践与社会空间的根本矛盾关联起来。陆兴华认为，"策展"作为一种内在的建筑行动来抵抗现行的建筑设计，因为在资本主义生产关系中的建筑设计与建筑师的美好理想始终是矛盾的，而策展就是摆脱这种纠缠的有效的反制手段。从某种程度上说，建筑师只有在策展之中才能真正实现他的设计作品。[3]197（图④）

When architects move from "design" to "curation", the space result is virtualized, turning a curatorial event into an ideal utopia. This is the demonstration that architects should give. This requires architects to curate the design space, which conforms to geometric and aesthetic rules, into social space, so that it can enter the production process of social space. It should be pointed out that as a discipline closely related to spatial practice, architecture and urban planning should certainly respond to the issue of space production. However, these explorations should be based on the premise of breaking away from the old disciplinary paradigm. The overall perspective of Lefebvre's *The Production of Space* may prompt the professionals of urban planning and architectural design to jump out of the narrow professional category and associate their thinking and practice with the fundamental contradiction of social space. Lu Xinghua believes that "Curation" is carried out as an internal architectural action to resist existing architectural design, because there is always a conflict between architectural design in the capitalist production relations and the architects' rosy ideal, and curation is just an effective means to get rid of this entanglement. To some extent, only in the curation can the architect truly realize his design works. [3]197 (Figure ④)

这绝不是说说而已，现在已经有人提出"离开建筑师原有的位置，用新的实践去创造建筑的意义"。在具体的行动实践中，建筑师与艺术家们以各自不同的方式对物理空间进行"再建"。《第一回无界建筑季：建筑，或者建筑》的策展人李巨川认为，建筑内部设计的公共空间仍然在等待着通过"再建"成为真正的公共空间。这也就是说，建筑物并不能解决今天的空间问题与居住问题，在已建成的建筑物环境中仍然需要"再建"。从这个意义上说，对一件作品的使用被看成是一个连续的过程，通过某种广泛多样的个人行为以及社会和制度实践而进行的一种价值的判断性运作。

This is by no means just empty talk, and now some people have put forward the idea of "leaving the original position of architects and creating the meaning of architecture with new practice". In practice, architects and artists have taken concrete actions to "rebuild" physical space in their respective ways. Li Juchuan, curator of "The First Borderless Architecture Season: Architecture, or Architecture", believes that the public space in the interior design of the building is still waiting to become real public space through "rebuilding". That is to say, buildings can not solve today's space and living problems, and still need to be "rebuilt" in the environment of completed buildings. In this sense, the use of a work is seen as a continuous process, a value-judging operation carried out through a wide variety of individual actions and social and institutional practices.

这里所说的"策展"已经摆脱了为了占有物质的那种紧张关系。作为和"策展"具有相同意义的"游戏"，情境主义国际关于它的定义是以消除商业竞争构式，建设一种临时性的、自由的流动式生命状态为目标的。在这些艺术家眼中，革命的游戏恰恰是打破商业化的日常生活规则的重要手段。从这个意义上说，何志森所进行的游戏情境，或者说所策划的展览，就是要让菜市场摊主从紧张的空间争夺中逃离出来，在临时游戏规则下使人复归人性的善良友好，共同创造无功利的美好天堂，也更加体现了"菜市场美术馆"的批判性特征。

The "curation" herein mentioned has got rid of the tension caused by material possession. "Game" has similar meaning as "curation" and is defined by Situationist International as a means to eliminate the commercial competition structure and to build a temporary, free and mobile state of life. In the eyes of these artists, revolutionary games are just an important means to break the rules of commercialized daily life. In this sense, the game situation, or the so-called exhibition curated by Jason Zhisen Ho, is to allow the stall owners to escape from the tense space competition, to restore the kindness and friendliness in human nature under the temporary rules of the game, and to create a non-utilitarian paradise, which further reflects the critical feature of Market Museum.

这已然不是建筑专家内部的游戏，而是一种实在的、具体的和每个人有关的建筑行动。需要强调的是，这种"策展"是"临时的"和"无功利的"：策展的内容并不对象化为客观存在，这种主体活动不像劳动生产或经济活动，它没有任何物性的实得，却在一种创造性场境活动和非支配的主客体关系中，让人的存在面向公平和正义。

This is no longer an internal game of architectural experts, but a real and concrete architectural action relevant to everyone. What needs to be emphasized is that this kind of "curation" is "temporary" and "non-utilitarian": the content of curation is not objectified as objective existence; this kind of subject activity is not like labor production or economic activity for it doesn't result in any material gain, but allows human beings to face fairness and justice in creative situational activities and non-dominant subject-object relationships.

由何志森发起的 Mapping 工作坊这一基于社会空间关系的乌托邦实践，不论是"菜市场美术馆"，还是之后的成都菽香里菜市场实验以及深圳桥头村人民公园改造，工作坊的项目使用的是一个从个体出发来探讨空间生产问题的策略——通过寻找通往新型空间的前路，他的探寻有意勾连科学与乌托邦、现实与理想、理论构想与生活实际。通过"可能"与"不可能"之间的辩证关系同时在客观和主观层面上进行探讨，何志森试图努力弥合每组对象中两者间的矛盾，以期待一种社会生活新形式和空间生产新方式的出现。

Mapping Workshop, a Utopian practice based on social spatial relations initiated by Jason Zhisen Ho, uses a strategy of exploring space production from individuals' point of view in projects ranging from the Market Museum, the subsequent Shuxiangli wet market experiment in Chengdu, to the renovation of the People's Park in Qiaotou Village, Shenzhen, to intentionally explore the links science and Utopia, reality and ideal, theoretical conception and life reality. By discussing the dialectical relationship between "possibility" and "impossibility" on both objective and subjective levels, Jason tries to bridge the contradiction between the two in each group of objects in order to expect the emergence of a new form of social life and a new way of space production.

笔者以为，未来的建筑师一半以上的工作需要考虑如何将其设计空间带入新的社会关系，他们的设计更多地是一种在社会中对空间作出的策展。这样的策展通过对社会关系的调整为现代性霸权空间重新打开一个可能世界的新视野，从而走向基于身体体验、艺术创造与城市革命的多种可能的、差异性的空间的生产。[4]

In my opinion, more than half of the work of architects in the future need to involve the integration of designed space with new social relations, and their design will be more like curatorial work on space in the society. By adjusting social relations, such curation re-opens a new horizon of a possible world for the hegemonic space of modernity, thus moving towards the production of various possible and different spaces based on physical experience, artistic creation and urban revolution. [4]

假使没有这种具有社会空间革命性质的策展，就不会有真正的社会主义新社会的实现，而空间的革命不在建筑学本体内部，它需要执业者的批判性和自发性，从"空间中的生产"转变为总体的"空间的生产"。"它首先向前看，需要执业者的批判性和自发性；它需要在消解自身学科边界的进程中超越自身，才有可能获得新的生命；它需要回到日常生活的批判性实践中，直面鲜活的社会现实和社会关系，在认识空间中的各种尖锐矛盾冲突中，同时在战略和战术两端工作，才不至于失去方向或陷入细碎和烦琐，进而在认识论的颠覆和创造性的实践中践行列斐伏尔的日常生活批判宣言。"[5]

Without such curation with revolutionary nature of social space, there will be no real realization of a new socialist society. But the revolution of space is not within architecture per se, it needs criticism and spontaneity of practitioners, and turn from "production in space" to overall "production of space". "It first looks forward and needs criticism and spontaneity of practitioners; It needs to transcend itself in the process of clearing up its own disciplinary boundaries in order to obtain a new life; It needs to return to the critical practice of daily life, face the vivid social reality and social relations, recognize the sharp contradictions and conflicts in the space, and at the same time, work at both strategic and tactical ends, so as not to lose direction or fall into detail and triviality, and then practice Lefebvre's critical declaration of daily life in the epistemological subversion and creative practice." [5]

3 "公众作为主体"
3 "The Public as Subject"

"菜市场美术馆"的真正价值不仅仅在于何志森对美术馆进行的"策展"，而是其将公众作为主体，让自己退居幕后。笔者以为这不仅是对摊贩和居民公共利益的维护，还有建筑师对自己和公众关系的审视。于是，一种让公众也成为建筑师的声音被呼唤出来："以民众为主体的空间创造才是真正讨论空间公共性的关键所在，那些没有受过建筑学训练的民众也是公共空间的生产者。真正让普通市民、环卫工人、外卖员和出租车司机等不同职业的人们加入到空间的再造中来。不同民众持续的占领和空间创作，利用手边的既有资源去建构属于他们自己的公共空间，使策划空间变成一个不同群体进行社会互动和交往的场所，让人们看到公民社会真正的核心价值。"[6]（图⑤）

The real value of Market Museum lies in not only Jason Zhisen Ho's "curation" of art museum, but also his making the public as subject and letting himself retreat behind the scenes, which I think is not only for the maintenance of the public interests of vendors and residents, but also reflects the architect's examination of the relationship between himself and the public. Therefore, a call for the public to become architects is voiced out: "The creation of space with the public as subject is the key to the real discussion of the publicness of space, and the people who have not received architectural training are also the producers of public space. We should really allow ordinary citizens including sanitation workers, deliverymen and taxi drivers from all walks of life to join in the rebuilding of space. The continuous occupation and space creation by various groups of people, using the existing resources at hand to construct their own public space, have made the curated space a place for different groups to interact and communicate, which allows people to see the real core values of a civil society." [6] (Figure ⑤)

⑤ 农林菜市场的摊主们（摄影：张雷）
The stall owners of the Nonglin Market (Photographer: Zhang Lei)

公众运用自身知识领域与生活经验的空间知识，在现有的城市空间缝隙里进行着人的空间创造与居住实践，抵抗着由权力所主导的空间生产。从这个视角看，公众也是一群新的建筑师主体。然而，这样的说法和做法似乎并不能得到建筑师或者社会大众的认可。这怎么是建筑师呢？如果真是这样的话，岂不是人人都是建筑师了？实际上，"人人都是建筑师"也正是笔者想表达和主张的，博伊斯（Joseph Beuys）早就告诉我们，人人都是艺术家，只要你愿意。但要明确的是，你愿意搞的艺术、建筑不是圈内和社会上通常理解的那种艺术、建筑，而是每个人自己的艺术和建筑。

The general public use the space knowledge in their own intellectual field and life experiences to carry out their respective space creation and living practice in the gaps of existing urban space, resisting the power-dominated space production. From this perspective, the public is also a new group of architects. However, such statements and practices do not seem to be recognized by architects or the public. How can they be architects? If it were so, wouldn't everyone else be an architect? In fact, that everyone is an architect is what I want to express and advocate. Joseph Beuys has long told us that everyone is an artist as long as he/she wants to. But it should be made clear that the art and architecture you are willing to engage in is not the kind of art and architecture usually understood in the professional circle and the society, but is everyone's own art and architecture.

坦白说，也并不是所有的建筑师、艺术家都能实现自己的理想，建筑师、艺术家也可能因为找不到活儿干而闷闷不乐，甚至面临被无产阶级化的窘境。与其这般挣扎和无奈，还不如思考、揭示一下其中蕴藏的奥秘。按照列斐伏尔的说法，基于图式、句法、艺术史式的观念理想空间，与城市居民的精神社会空间有着本质的区别。建筑师生产出来的是抽象空间，抽象空间是一种资本主义的政治经济空间，是由资本主义国家干预和支配的空间，最终形成同质化、碎片化、等级化的资本主义空间特征。可能连柯布西耶也没有想到，他以功能主义范式建造起来的都市空间竟成了资本追逐利润的主要方式。

Frankly speaking, not all architects and artists can realize their ideals. They may also be unhappy when they lose their jobs or even face the dilemma of proletarianization. Instead of being trapped in such struggling and helplessness, it is better to think and reveal the hidden mysteries. According to Lefebvre, conceptual ideal space based on schema, syntax and art history is essentially different from the spiritual social space of urban residents. What architects produce is abstract space, which is a kind of capitalist political and economic space. It is intervened and dominated by capitalist countries, and ultimately forms such characteristics of capitalist space as homogenization, fragmentation and hierarchy. Perhaps even Corbusier would not expect that the urban space he built with the paradigm of functionalism has become the major means for capital to pursue profits.

然而，他们也想将某种社会、哲学视野坚持到底，比如，要求根据"人的感受和需求""为人民而建"等，也使用列斐伏尔、德波的话语来表达自己的正义，并将自己看作是新社会关系的创造者。而建筑评论家们也一再为这种空间赋予这样或那样的意义，但依然是枉费心机，塔夫里早也指出了这一点。

However, they also want to stick to a certain social and philosophical vision to the end, e.g., conforming to "human feelings and needs" "built for the people", and so on. They also use Lefebvre's and Debord's words to express their justice, and regard themselves as the creators of new social relations. Although architectural critics have repeatedly given such space this or that kind of meaning, it's still in vain, as Tafuri had pointed out earlier.

按照法国社会学家皮埃尔·布迪厄（Pierre Bourdieu）对经济资本与文化资本的区分，我们认识到知识分子在社会中处于统治与被统治并存的矛盾地位。作为中产知识分子的建筑师的品味判断与社会地位也能造成社会生活中的权力关系——一方面要服务甲方，另一方面又要承担道义与社会责任。是不是很纠结？即使是大咖，他们的良好意愿也是大打折扣了的，只要在权力与资本的安排和管控下，建筑师的创作也就不可避免地异化了公众的生活，剥夺了公众对空间的权力。

According to the distinction made by French sociologist Pierre Bourdieu between economic capital and cultural capital, we realize that intellectuals are in a contradictory position owing to the coexistence of their dominating and being dominated statuses in society. As middle-class intellectuals, architects' taste judgment and social status can also cause power relations in social life—on the one hand, they need to serve Party A; on the other, to assume moral and social responsibilities. Would these two forces tear them apart? Even master architects have to compromise their good will. As long as it's under the arrangement and control of power and capital, architects' creation will inevitably alienate the public's life and deprive them of their power over space.

今天的建筑设计仍然被认为是一种只有少数人才能完成的人类活动，那些设计出独特空间的建筑师都是训练有素的"天才"。列斐伏尔告诉我们，必须克服空间作为独特的作品和空间作为产品的商品的分离。也就是说，建筑师不应该拿自己作品的独特来说事。"你"独特的作品和"我"有什么关系呢？"我"要的是和"我"权益紧密相关的作品，哪怕只是一个摊位、一张照片、一件可以坐一会儿吸支烟的废旧家具。这种由人人构建起的各种情境，就是德波说的"那些能够确定一个时刻和质量的集体环境"。

Architectural design today is still regarded as a human activity that only a few people can accomplish, and those architects who design unique spaces are well-trained geniuses. Lefebvre tells us that the separation of space as unique work and space as commodity product must be overcome. That is to say, architects should not boast of the uniqueness of their work—"your" unique work has nothing to do with "me". What "I" want is the work that's closely related to "my" rights and interests, even if it is only a booth, a photo, a piece of old furniture that can sit for a while and smoke a cigarette. These various kinds of situation constructed by everyone is what Debord calls "the collective environment that can determine a moment and the quality".

那么，公众就务必将自己生活革命化的能力发挥出来，可惜，公众在今天也已成为看客，不能被称作演员。作为建筑师，帮助公众解放自己不是要将他理解的东西强加给公众，而是要鼓励公众讲他们自己的建筑故事。（图⑥）

Therefore, the public must tap into their potential to revolutionize their own life. Unfortunately, the public today have become spectators and can't be called actors. For architects, helping the public to liberate themselves is not to impose their own understanding on the public, but to encourage the public to tell their own architectural stories. (Figure ⑥)

遗憾的是，当下拥有"空间正义"的建筑师热衷于替代公众发声，他们常说他们要为公众怎样怎样。当然，我们不能无视建筑师的情怀，但问题在于建筑师按自己的意图剪裁表述而不顾它们与"空间的生产"的三元整体关联。建筑师对"正义空间"的阐释实际上是以索亚（Edward W.Soja）创造性误读出"第三空间"[4]为理论基础的。[5]

⑥ 菜市场被拆之后，摊主将"手"的照片悬挂在街头
After the market was demolished, a stall owner hung the picture of her hands in the street

Unfortunately, the current architects who own "space justice" are keen to voice out on behalf of the public. They often talk about they want to do this or that for the public. Of course, we should not ignore the respectful sentiments of architects, but the problem is that architects tailor their expressions according to their own intentions, regardless of the three-dimensional overall association with "the production of space". In fact, architects' interpretation of "justice space" is theoretically based on Edward W. Soja's creative misreading of "the third space" [4] [5]

当然，这也是现代建筑史上遗留下来的产物，就像塔夫里认为的那样，建筑师拥有天生的形而上学合法性，公众只是在建筑师作品内涵方面起关键作用的译者而非作者。目前的"建筑评奖""建筑批评"的导向也依然是以专家学者的话语权为基础的，也是简易和安全的专业评审。专家学者较少将公众的意见考虑在内，他们认为建筑评论与公众没有太大关系，也无法有太大关系；反之，公众对于建筑问题的意见也难得到专业共同体的认同和许可。与"建筑畅言网"发起的"建筑评选"活动采用大众与专家相结合的评选方式相比，可能是因为"公众的素质参差不齐"，也可能是"不好操作"，这届三联人文城市奖的评选缺少了公众参与这一环节。

Of course, this is also a legacy of modern architecture history. As believed by Tafuri, architects have an innate metaphysical legitimacy, and the public is the translator rather than the author who plays a key role in interpreting the connotation of architects' works. At present, the orientation of "architectural awards" and "architectural criticism" is still based on the discourse power of experts and scholars, which is indeed simple and safe professional review. Experts and scholars don't often take public opinion into account for they think that architectural criticism has little or nothing to do with the public. On the other hand, the public's opinions on architectural issues are hardly respected by the professional community. Different from the selection approach by "Architecture Selection" campaign launched by "Network of Free Speech on Architecture", which includes both the public and experts in the panel, this year's Sanlian City for Humanity Awards did not include the tache of public participation, which may be due to "uneven quality of the public" or "difficult operation".

在现代社会里,"公众参与"毕竟是一个漂亮的说法,关于公众与专家的关系有着迥然不同的见解。为了达成专业内外的交流形成共赢局面,有不少学者给出了自己的见解。无论在怎样的意见中,多数专家都认为需要提高全民审美修养,以便他们可以跟得上建筑师的品位。但也有人认为:"要让建筑成为公共议题的途径并不在于对公众进行普及型的建筑教育,而取决于当代建筑实践和评论是否有回归当下社会经验现实的勇气与决心。"[7] 这一观点似乎暗合了布迪厄言及的反对宰制群体和被宰制群体的区隔,以消解文化精英所主导的纯粹美学和庸俗美学的社会建构。

In modern society, "public participation" is something that would win applause after all, and there are diverse opinions about the relationship between the public and experts. In order to achieve a win-win situation in exchanges between professional and the public, many scholars have given their own opinions. Whatever the opinion is, most experts agree that it is necessary to improve the aesthetic cultivation of the general public so that they can keep up with the taste of architects. However, some people believe that "the way to make architecture a public topic is not to conduct universal education of architecture, but depends on whether contemporary architectural practice and criticism have the courage and determination to return to the reality of current social experience".[7] This view seems to coincide with the distinction between the anti-dominant group and the dominated group mentioned by Bourdieu, which aims at eliminating the social construction of pure aesthetics and vulgar aesthetics dominated by cultural elites.

布迪厄提出，大众审美观对于建构它的社会群体而言是真实的、有意义的，因而不能被贬低为高雅美学的"陪衬"。从公众的角度来说，他们肯定不像建筑师那样了解建筑，事实上也无需像建筑师那样去了解建筑。有学者认为，建筑师和公众的对话不是建立在建筑的专业道理上的，而是需要在"一般道理的特殊经验"上来探讨。[6] 在此情形下，大家才能依据自身的认知能力和主观状况谈论对建筑的看法，用评论者个人的理性而非教条来进行评论，进一步用他们个人的行动来批评建筑实践及建筑师们的话语。

Burdieu claimed that mass aesthetics is real and meaningful for the social groups that construct it, so it can not be belittled as a "foil" to highbrow aesthetics. From the public's point of view, they certainly do not understand architecture as architects do; in fact, they do not need to understand architecture as architects do. Some scholars believe that the dialogue between architects and the public is not based on the professional theory of architecture, but on "the particular experience of general theory".[6] In this case, people can talk about their views on architecture according to their own cognitive ability and subjective situation, comment with their own rationality rather than dogmas, and further criticize architectural practice and architects' discourse with their own actions.

对于希望真正解决问题的人来说，我们需要努力把握总体的内容，而不是孤立地去实现几个碎片化的梦想。列斐伏尔告诉我们，总体的异化实践需要总体的反异化实践来克服，他将马克思式的"总体的人"变成尼采式的"超人"，从而走向了挣脱一切羁绊的理想境界。在列斐伏尔的总体的人理想视野中，"总体的人是自由集体中的自由的个人，它是在差别无穷的各种可能性的个性中充分发展的个性。"[8] 人的本性源自艺术的自由创造，因为具有永恒价值与魅力的艺术始终包含着一种走向总体行动的努力。这就是说，"总体的人"的主要形式是一种艺术——这是一种在日常生活艺术化过程中实现人类自我解放的艺术乌托邦。

For those who want to really solve the problem, we need to strive to grasp the overall content, rather than to realize several fragmented dreams in isolation. Lefebvre tells us that the practice of overall alienation needs to be overcome by the practice of overall anti-alienation and he turns the Marxian "total man" into the Nietzschean "superman", thus moving towards the ideal state of breaking away from all fetters. In Lefebvre's ideal vision of the total man, "the total man is a free individual in a free collective, and it is a fully developed personality among all the personalities of various possibilities with infinite differences". [8] Human nature comes from the free creation of art, because art with eternal value and charm always contains an effort to move towards a total action. That is to say, the main form of "total man" is a kind of art, which is an artistic Utopia to realize human self-liberation in the process of making daily life artistic.

从这个意义上说，人人都有权利来理解、设计空间，一旦以平等的姿态参与实践，公众就可以自己来"居有"作品。当菜市场美术馆的摊贩们将手的照片拿回到菜市场，挂在自己的摊位上时，菜市场就成为一个美术馆：有人在她的《豆腐美术馆》前面摆放灯牌，有人在她的鸡肉档旁放了一个循环播放卡通小鸡视频的电视……在他们看来，这就是艺术作品，这就是他们的居有空间。遗憾的是，在重庆悦来美术馆"向下生活里的X种空间方案"的展览中，何志森取代摊主变成了参展建筑师，他没能再次让摊主成为作品的创造者，而以"致敬"的名义将摊主当成了演员。事实上，要做到每一次都让公众作为主体真的很难，需要建筑师细致甄别以公众为主体的界限并以极大的勇气和耐心面对每一个人的真实需求。

In this sense, everyone has the right to understand and design space. Once participating in the practice with an equal attitude, the public can come to "own" their works. When the vendors of the Market Museum take their photos back to the wet market and hang them on their stalls, the market becomes an art museum: someone put a lighted signboard in front of her *Tofu Art Museum*, someone put a TV next to her chicken stall that played a looping cartoon chicken video…In their eyes, these are works of art and the space they own. Unfortunately, in the exhibition "X Kinds of Space Schemes in Downward Life" in Chongqing Yuelai Art Museum, Jason replaced the stall owners as the participating architect, and failed to make the stall owners the creators of the works again; instead, the stall owners were regarded as actors in the name of "tribute". In fact, it is really difficult to make the public as the main body every time, which requires careful examination of the boundaries of the public as the main body as well as great courage and patience to face every individual's real needs.

4 小结
4 Conclusion

今年 9 月底，我收到扉美术馆工作人员从广州寄来的一包土壤和十粒葵花种子。我随即按照"说明"，在废旧容器里倒进泥土，并将种子埋了起来。没有太过精心地养护，国庆节的时候，嫩芽竟然冒了出来并且一天天长大。这一过程给我庸常的生活带来了乐趣，用尼采的话来说就是"瞬间"的打开，让我的生活有种超越当下的欢愉力量。与此同时，我作为一名从业者第一次参加了"展览"，实现了我的"行动"成为"作品"的理想，我的自豪感也油然而生。从这个意义上说，何志森又进行了一次列斐伏尔意义上的社会空间的"策展"。正如前文所指出的，这种策展与把艺术作品摆到美术馆里让观众参观的那种不同，也与"社区花园"那种对城市空间的治理方式不同，它通过"不造物"的方式让每一个普通人参与到关于塑造空间、美化生活的事件中来，不分时间和地点，具有无限的广度和深度。我以为，这是一件具有"后当代艺术"意义的作品，也就是说，它比当代艺术还要当代，是今天社会走向公平、正义、和谐，人民群众实现美好生活愿景的一次艺术的总体性动员。（图⑦）

At the end of September this year, I received a bag of soil and ten sunflower seeds from the staff of the FEI Arts in Guangzhou. I immediately poured soil into the waste container and buried the seeds in it according to the "instruction". Without extra care and nurturing, during the National Day Holiday, the buds unexpectedly came out and grew day by day. This process has brought enjoyment to my ordinary daily life which, in Nietzsche's words, "instantly" opened up my life to a force of joy that transcends the present. At the same time, as a practitioner, I participated in the "exhibition" for the first time, and realized my ideal of turning "action" into "work", which made my heart burst with pride. In this sense, Jason Zhisen Ho once again carried out a "curation" of social space in Lefebvre's way. As mentioned above, this kind of curation is different from the usual placement of artworks in galleries for visitors to view, and also different from People's Garden's way of governing urban space; instead, it allows every ordinary person to participate in the event of shaping the space and beautifying their life through the way of "non-creation", regardless of time and place, and with infinite breadth and depth. In my opinion, this is a work with the significance of post-contemporary art. In other words, it is more contemporary than contemporary art. It is an overall mobilization of art for today's society to move towards fairness, justice and harmony, and for the people to realize the vision of a better life. (Figure ⑦)

⑦ 菜市场摊主们拿着"手"的照片的合影
A group photo of the vendors holding a picture of their hands

只有这样,人们才能摆脱各种束缚,克服与超越日常生活的异化走向快乐空间的生产。何志森作为"策展人"给我们树立了这样的榜样——建筑师从陶醉于"文脉""句法""样式"的空间生产走向"游戏""架构""策展"的空间社会关系的再生产。当然,这样的情境需要构建在物质和精神都非常富足的基础上,今天的中国具备这样的条件了吗? 如果具备了,那这样做是否是将传统建筑师的职业消解了呢? 笔者认为并没有,这需要我们怀着的是改造社会和改造世界的理想,而不是只把设计房子当成一个实现个人理想和艺术追求的职业。

Only in this way can people get rid of all kinds of constraints, overcome and transcend the alienation of daily life and move towards the production of happy space. Jason Zhisen Ho, as a "curator", has set such an exemplar for us—the architect is no longer intoxicated with the production of space in terms of "context", "syntax" and "style", but moves towards the reproduction of socio-spatial relations in terms of "game", "structure" and "curation". Of course, such a landscape needs to be built on the basis of material and spiritual prosperity. Is China equipped with such conditions today? If so, would the profession of architecture be eliminated? I don't think so. However, we should cherish the ideal of making the society and the world better, instead of regarding design of house as merely a profession to realize one's personal ideal and artistic pursuit.

注释 Notes

1） 何志森. 边界是个机会 [J/OL]. 建筑档案，[2021-3-15]. https://www.thepaper.cn/newsDetail_forward_11728025
Jason Zhisen Ho. Boundary is an Opportunity [J/OL]. Architectural Archives, [2021-3-15]. https://www.thepaper.cn/newsDetail_forward_11728025

2） 什么是当下的城市人文，城市中国杂志 [EB/OL]. [2021-4-14]. http://www.guihuayun.com/read/70191
What Is the Current Urban Humanities, Urban China Magazine [EB/OL]. [2021-4-144]. http://www.guihuayun.com/read/70191

3） 地质学家们的工作已经给我们很好的提示：人类以及人类居住于其上的地球进入一个新的纪元了。这不仅是一个很好的提示，而且已经给出了一个充分的证据，足以让我们在哲学上更系统地、更深刻地理解技术的本质和人类的未来。哲学应当比地质学更进一步深入到人类生活和文化的层面来追问和探讨。见：孙周兴. 人类世的哲学 [M]. 北京：商务印书馆，2020：8，99.
Geologists tell us that human beings and the earth they inhabit have entered a new era, which allows people to understand the nature of technology and the future of human beings. Philosophy should go deeper than geology to question and explore on the level of human life and culture more systematically and profoundly. Quoted from: Sun Zhouxing. Philosophy of the Anthropocene [M]. Beijing: Commercial Press, 2020:8,99.

4） 第三空间既是物质也是精神的开放空间，建构第三空间的步骤是"他者化—第三化"，从"第一"到"第三"意味着空间生产的序列性和等级性。
The third space is an open space both materially and spiritually. The steps of constructing the third space are "other—third". From "first" to "third" means the sequence and hierarchy of space production.

5） 索亚试图将列斐伏尔的空间理论解读成一种空间本体论，这种解读是对列斐伏尔的空间概念的误解。见：杨舢. "空间生产"话语在英美与中国的传播历程及其在中国城市规划与地理学领域的误读 [J]. 国际城市规划，2021（3）：35.
Soja tries to interpret Lefebvre's space theory as a kind of space ontology, which is a misunderstanding of Lefebvre's concept of space. For details, please refer to Yang Yun. The Propagation Course of the Discourse of "Space Production" in Britain, USA and China and Its Misunderstanding in the Fields of Urban Planning and Geography in China [J]. International Urban Planning, 2021(3): 35.

6） 陈嘉映. 不懂建筑的人能不能谈建筑的道理？ [J/OL]. 第一哲学家，[2021-2-16]. https://mp.weixin.qq.com/s/cIbyBZ97W74U5yRpYwa1uQ
Chen Jiayin. Can Laypeople Talk About the Principles of Architecture? [J/OL]. First Philosopher, [2021-2-16]. https://mp.weixin.qq.com/s/cIbyBZ97W74U5yRpYwa1uQ

参考文献 Reference

[1] [法] 让 – 弗朗索瓦·利奥塔. 异识 [M]. 上海：上海文艺出版社，2022（3）：5.
[France] Jean-Francois Lyotard. The Differend [M]. Shanghai: Shanghai Literature and Art Publishing House, 2022 (3): 5.

[2] 刘怀玉. 现代性的平庸与神奇——列斐伏尔日常生活批判哲学的文本学解读 [M]. 北京：北京师范大学出版社，2018（8）：417.
Liu Huaiyu. The Mediocrity and Magic of Modernity: A Textual Interpretation of Lefebvre's Critical Philosophy of Everyday Life [M]. Beijing: Beijing Normal University Press. 2018(8):417.

[3] 陆兴华. 人类世与平台城市：城市哲学 1[M]. 南京：南京大学出版社，2021.
Lu Xinghua. Anthropocene and Platform City: Urban Philosophy 1[M]. Nanjing: Nanjing University Press, 2021.

[4] 刘怀玉. 简论"空间的生产"之内在辩证关系及其三重意义 [J]. 国际城市规划，2021（3）：20.
Liu Huaiyu. On the Inner Dialectical Relationship and Its Triple Significance of "Space Production" [J]. International City Planning, 2021(3):20.

[5] 杨宇振. 日常生活批判宣言：亨利·列斐伏尔的"空间生产"理论关键线索 [J]. 时代建筑，2021（4）：22.
Yang Yuzhen. Critical Manifesto of Everyday Life: Key Clues of Henri Lefebvre's Theory of Space Production [J]. Time Architecture, 2021(4):22.

[6] 何志森. 从人民公园到人民的公园 [J]. 建筑学报，2020（11）：28.
Jason Zhisen Ho. From People's Park to the Park of the People [J]. Journal of Architecture, 2020(11): 28.

[7] 周榕. 走向"新批评"——当代建筑评论的价值体认、智识分工与任务定位 [J]. 建筑学报，2020（11）：10.
Zhou Rong. Towards New Criticism: Value Recognition, Intellectual Division and Task Orientation of Contemporary Architectural Criticism [J]. Journal of Architecture, 2020(11):10.

[8] Henri Lefebvre. Dialectical Materialism[M]. J.Sturrock translation, London:Jonathan Cape, 1968:163.

奖项·展览
Awards and Exhibitions

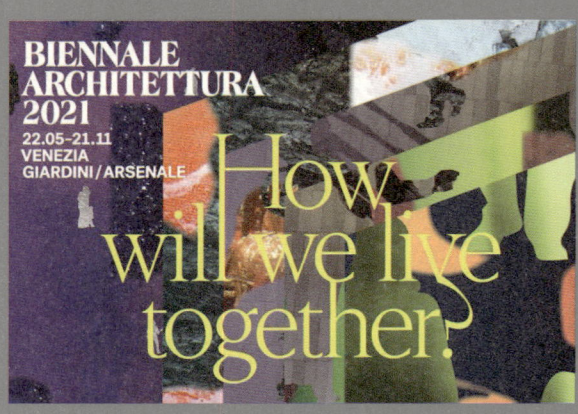

2021 年威尼斯建筑双年展官方海报,主题"我们将如何共同生活?"
The official poster of the Venice Architecture Biennale 2021 titled "How will we live together?"

获奖

2022	获日本优良设计奖 （紫泥十二门无界社区）	
2021	获国际风景园林师协会（IFLA）亚太区年度杰出大奖 （菜市场美术馆）	
2021	入围 ArchDaily 2021 中国建筑榜单前 10 名 （紫泥十二门无界社区）	
2020	获中国建筑奖（WAACA）居住贡献奖佳作奖 （紫泥十二门无界社区）	
2020	获 ADA 年度亚洲设计大奖之居住建筑与空间类型——思考与探索奖 （紫泥十二门无界社区）	
2020	获三联人文城市奖——社区营造范例 （菜市场美术馆）	
2020	入选 Dezeen 2020 年中国十大建筑榜单 （紫泥十二门无界社区）	
2020	Dezeen Awards 年度最佳住宅大奖 （紫泥十二门无界社区）	
2020	WAN Awards 综合体建筑 MIXED USE 金奖 （紫泥十二门无界社区）	
2020	RICS（皇家特许测量师协会）中国奖年度城市更新项目 （紫泥十二门无界社区）	

展览

2022	第四届中国设计大展暨公共艺术专题展，中国 深圳 （紫泥十二门无界社区、菜市场美术馆）
2021	第四届深圳当代艺术双年展，中国 深圳 （菜市场美术馆）
2021	弹性社区，意大利 佛罗伦萨 （菜市场美术馆）
2021	"向下生活里的 X 种空间方案"，中国 重庆 （菜市场美术馆）
2021	第 17 届威尼斯建筑双年展（意大利国家馆），意大利 威尼斯 （菜市场美术馆）
2019	CADE 建筑设计博览会，中国 上海 （紫泥十二门无界社区）
2019	"内部性与外部性——工业遗产改造再利用"，中国 深圳 （紫泥十二门无界社区）
2019	"中国新建筑——20 位筑造未来的女性"，中国 上海 （紫泥十二门无界社区）

文章

1 汪原. 互联网时代的"社会冷凝器"——紫泥堂纤维板厂改造设计的意义 [J]. 建筑学报, 2019（613）: 92–97.

2 刘小康. 无界生活的无界居所: 广州紫泥堂纤维板厂改造项目的解读 [J]. 时代建筑, 2019（03）: 138–143.

3 米笑. 竹丝岗, 一座不断生长的无界博物馆 [J]. 建筑学报, 2019（610）: 19–23.

4 Richard J. Weller, Tatum L. Hands. Market, or Museum?[M] . Beautiful China: Reflections on Landscape Architecture in Contemporary China, ORO Editions, 2020.

5 辛塞波. "走向策展"和"公众主体"的菜市场美术馆 [J]. 公共艺术, 2021（03）: 102–107.

Major Awards

2022	GOOD DESIGN AWARD 2022 (Borderless Community of Zi Ni Twelve Portals)	
2021	Outstanding Award of IFLA ASIA-PAC LA Awards 2021 (Market Museum)	
2021	Top 10 projects of ArchDaily China's Building of the Year 2021 Awards (Borderless Community of Zi Ni Twelve Portals)	
2020	Outstanding Residential Design Award of WAACA (Borderless Community of Zi Ni Twelve Portals)	
2020	Thinking and Exploration Award of ADA Annual Asian Design Award—Residential Building and Space Award (Borderless Community of Zi Ni Twelve Portals)	
2020	City for Humanity Awards Example of Community Empowerment (Market Museum)	
2020	China's Top 10 Buildings of Dezeen Awards 2020 (Borderless Community of Zi Ni Twelve Portals)	
2020	Winner (Housing Project) of Dezeen Awards 2020 (Borderless Community of Zi Ni Twelve Portals)	
2020	Gold Award (Mixed Use) of WAN Awards 2020 (Borderless Community of Zi Ni Twelve Portals)	
2020	Excellence Award (Regeneration Project) of RICS (Royal Institute of Chartered Surveyors) China Awards 2020 (Borderless Community of Zi Ni Twelve Portals)	

Exhibitions

2022	The 4th China Design Exhibition cum Public Art Exhibition in Shenzhen, China (Borderless Community of Zi Ni Twelve Portals, The Market Museum)
2021	The 4th Shenzhen Contemporary Art Biennale, Shenzhen, China (Market Museum)
2021	Paesaggi Resilienti per Comunità Resilienti, Florence, Italy (Market Museum)
2021	"X Kinds of Space Schemes in Downward Life", Chongqing, China (Market Museum)
2021	The 17th Venice Architecture Biennale (Italian National Expo), Venice, Italy (Market Museum)
2019	China Architecture Design Expo (CADE) 2019, Shanghai, China (Borderless Community of Zi Ni Twelve Portals)
2019	"Internality and Externality Transformation & Reuse of Industrial Heritage", Shenzhen, China (Borderless Community of Zi Ni Twelve Portals)
2019	"China's New Architecture 20 Women Building the Future", Shanghai, China (Borderless Community of Zi Ni Twelve Portals)

Articles

1 Wang Yuan. The "Social Condenser" in the Age of Internet–The Significance of the Renovation of Zi Ni Tang Fiberboard Factory[J]. Journal of Architecture, 2019 (613):92-97.

2 Liu Xiaokang. Borderless House for Borderless Life: The Interpretation of Zi Ni Tang Fiberboard Factory Renovation[J]. Times Architecture, 2019(03):138-143.

3 Michelle Yip. Zhusigang, a Growing Borderless Museum[J]. Journal of Architecture, 2019(610):19-23.

4 Richard J. Weller, Tatum L. Hands. Market, or Museum?[M]. Beautiful China: Reflections on Landscape Architecture in Contemporary China, ORO Editions, 2020

5 Xin Saibo. The Market Museum "Moving Towards Curation" and "with Public as Subject"[J]. Public Art, 2021(03):102-107.

扉建筑作品目录（2006—2022）
FEI Architects Projects List 2006—2022

1　亿达大厦
　　地点：广东 广州
　　时间：2005—2006 年
　　规模：11312.5 平方米
　　状态：建成
　　业主：恒满房地产置业有限公司

2　喜迎门展厅
　　地点：广东 广州
　　时间：2007 年
　　规模：1370 平方米
　　状态：建成
　　业主：广州喜迎门装饰设计工程有限公司

3　保安前街八号会馆
　　地点：广东 广州
　　时间：2006—2008 年
　　规模：152 平方米
　　状态：建成
　　业主：恒满房地产置业有限公司

4　天英茶业（正佳广场店）
　　地点：广东 广州
　　时间：2006 年
　　规模：39 平方米
　　状态：建成
　　业主：中山市天英茶业有限公司

5　广州丽柏广场室内设计
　　地点：广东 广州
　　时间：2007 年
　　规模：540 平方米
　　状态：建成
　　业主：广州君翊房地产发展有限公司

6　广州市城市规划设计所办公室
　　地点：广东 广州
　　时间：2007 年
　　规模：370 平方米
　　状态：建成
　　业主：广州市城市规划设计所

7　广州烟尘治理专业有限公司改造
　　地点：广东 广州
　　时间：2007—2009 年
　　规模：10000 平方米
　　状态：建成
　　业主：广州烟尘治理专业有限公司

8　广州国汇保险经纪有限公司办公室
　　地点：广东 广州
　　时间：2007 年
　　规模：408 平方米
　　状态：建成
　　业主：广州国汇保险经纪有限公司

9　扉美术馆
　　地点：广东 广州
　　时间：2007/2009/2016 年
　　规模：450 平方米
　　状态：建成
　　业主：满堂红（中国）置业有限公司

10　广州文华东方酒店办公室室内设计
　　地点：广东 广州
　　时间：2008—2011 年
　　规模：4000 平方米
　　状态：建成
　　业主：太古汇（广州）发展有限公司

11　武汉"保利心语"室内设计
　　地点：湖北 武汉
　　时间：2008 年
　　规模：4000 平方米
　　状态：建成
　　业主：保利（武汉）房地产开发有限公司

12　保利·西子湾室内设计
　　地点：广东 广州
　　时间：2008 年
　　规模：266.94 平方米
　　状态：建成
　　业主：保利房地产（集团）股份有限公司

13　广州岭南国际企业集团办公总部
　　地点：广东 广州
　　时间：2008—2009 年
　　规模：4200 平方米
　　状态：建成
　　业主：广州岭南国际企业集团有限公司

14　北京北奥艺通文化艺术发展有限公司
　　地点：广东 广州
　　时间：2008—2009 年
　　规模：1200 平方米
　　状态：方案设计
　　业主：北京北奥艺通文化艺术发展有限公司

1　　9

3

14　15

19

21

22

15 太古汇·汇坊
地点：广东 广州
时间：2008—2009 年
规模：10200 平方米
状态：建成
业主：堡泉（广州）物业管理有限公司

16 第 16 届亚运会开闭幕式创意团队办公室
地点：广东 广州
时间：2009 年
规模：200 平方米
状态：建成
业主：北京北奥艺通文化艺术发展有限公司

17 珠江新城核心区集中供冷中心地面建筑
地点：广东 广州
时间：2009 年
规模：150 平方米
状态：建成
业主：立信集团

18 "广州第一染织厂"餐饮项目室内设计
地点：广东 广州
时间：2010 年
规模：10000 平方米
状态：方案设计
业主：广州市逸越企业发展有限公司

19 成都石象湖雅乐轩酒店
地点：四川 成都
时间：2010—2015 年
规模：13203 平方米
状态：建成
业主：保利（成都）石象湖旅游发展有限公司

20 保利阳江银滩室内设计
地点：广东 阳江
时间：2010—2011 年
规模：1998 平方米
状态：建成
业主：保利（海陵岛）房地产开发有限公司

21 二沙文立方
地点：广东 广州
时间：2010—2018 年
规模：22550 平方米
状态：建成
业主：广东晴波投资有限公司

22 鸣泉居国宾馆
地点：广东 广州
时间：2010 年
规模：3963 平方米
状态：建成
业主：广州市鸣泉居度假村有限公司

23 例外·方所
地点：广东 广州
时间：2010—2011 年
规模：1600 平方米
状态：建成
业主：珠海建轩服饰有限公司

24 四海一家成都店室内设计
地点：四川 成都
时间：2010 年
规模：2500 平方米
状态：建成
业主：广州市番禺区南村四海一家美食城

25 流行美——首发空间
地点：广东 广州
时间：2011—2012 年
规模：515 平方米
状态：建成
业主：广州市流行美商业有限公司

26 四海寒舍
地点：广东 广州
时间：2011—2013 年
规模：3311 平方米
状态：建成
业主：广州市四海一家旅游开发有限公司

27 广东时代美术馆咖啡书店
地点：广东 广州
时间：2011—2012 年
规模：415 平方米
状态：建成
业主：广东时代美术馆

28 荔湾文化休闲区重点地段改造
地点：广东 广州
时间：2011 年
状态：方案设计
业主：广州市城市规划勘测设计研究院

23

26

27

28

31

34

29　鹤山市云乡寒舍建筑及室内设计
　　地点：广东 鹤山
　　时间：2011 年
　　规模：2000 平方米
　　状态：方案设计
　　业主：鹤山市天英生态园有限公司

30　手牵手环江幼稚园
　　地点：广西 河池
　　时间：2011—2013 年
　　规模：1945 平方米
　　状态：建成
　　业主：手牵手

31　香港理工大学艺术馆及校友活动中心
　　地点：香港 九龙
　　时间：2012 年
　　规模：500 平方米
　　状态：方案设计
　　业主：香港理工大学

32　琶洲叁悦广场写字楼室内设计
　　地点：广东 广州
　　时间：2012—2014 年
　　规模：5468 平方米
　　状态：建成
　　业主：保利房地产（集团）股份有限公司

33　叠院——莱蒙富阳别墅区室内设计
　　地点：江西 南昌
　　时间：2012—2014 年
　　规模：198 平方米，250 平方米
　　状态：方案设计
　　业主：莱蒙置业（富阳）有限公司

34　星海音乐厅大堂改造
　　地点：广东 广州
　　时间：2012—2013 年
　　规模：793 平方米
　　状态：建成
　　业主：广东省星海音乐厅

35　美尚美服装城
　　地点：广东 广州
　　时间：2012 年
　　规模：12000 平方米
　　状态：方案设计
　　业主：四季风尚

36　旧村改造 × 艺术拾遗——琶洲村综合体项目
　　地点：广东 广州
　　时间：2012—2016 年
　　规模：1200 平方米
　　状态：建成
　　业主：保利房地产（集团）股份有限公司

37　广州市琶洲村改造思亲楼建筑设计
　　地点：广东 广州
　　时间：2014 年
　　规模：1416 平方米
　　状态：建成
　　业主：保利房地产（集团）股份有限公司

38　保利龙门林语花园度假别墅
　　地点：广东 惠州
　　时间：2013 年
　　规模：368 平方米
　　状态：方案设计
　　业主：惠州生活之原旅游开发有限公司

39　上杭金马大酒店
　　地点：福建 上杭
　　时间：2013—2015 年
　　规模：43472 平方米
　　状态：方案设计
　　业主：福建金马大酒店有限公司

40　华安达实业公司广晟国际大厦写字楼室内设计
　　地点：广东 广州
　　时间：2013 年
　　规模：800 平方米
　　状态：建成
　　业主：广州市华安达实业有限公司

41　扉建筑
　　地点：广东 广州
　　时间：2013 年
　　规模：395 平方米
　　状态：建成
　　业主：广州扉越建筑设计事务所有限公司

42　云居——中山大红袍山庄
　　地点：广东 中山
　　时间：2013—2014 年
　　规模：31269 平方米
　　状态：方案设计
　　业主：天英实业

36—37

40

41

42

47

51

43 星海音乐厅系列改造——小厅
　　地点：广东 广州
　　时间：2014—2015 年
　　规模：345 平方米
　　状态：建成
　　业主：广东省星海音乐厅

44 保利珠海天悦样板间室内设计
　　地点：广东 珠海
　　时间：2014—2015 年
　　规模：189.79 平方米
　　状态：建成
　　业主：珠海保利天悦投资控股有限公司

45 莱蒙南昌商业项目外立面设计
　　地点：江西 南昌
　　时间：2014—2015 年
　　规模：110000 平方米
　　状态：建成
　　业主：南昌莱蒙置业有限公司

46 键盘
　　地点：广东 广州
　　时间：2014 年
　　规模：W3000 毫米 ×L3000 毫米
　　状态：建成
　　业主：保利房地产（集团）股份有限公司

47 琶洲精品酒店
　　地点：广东 广州
　　时间：2014 年
　　规模：12460 平方米
　　状态：方案设计
　　业主：保利房地产（集团）股份有限公司

48 那吉温泉别墅
　　地点：广东 恩平
　　时间：2014 年
　　规模：5124 平方米
　　状态：方案设计
　　业主：恩平市金汤旅游开发有限公司

49 中山大学模范村 508 楼、510 楼改造
　　地点：广东 广州
　　时间：2014 年
　　状态：方案设计
　　业主：中山大学

50 茶文化棋珍荟外立面改造
　　地点：广东 广州
　　时间：2014 年
　　规模：7025 平方米
　　状态：方案设计
　　业主：广州市羚羊投资咨询有限公司

51 保安前街 6 号
　　地点：广东 广州
　　时间：2014—2017 年
　　规模：453.01 平方米
　　状态：建成
　　业主：广东邦华集团有限公司

52 《生活美学》杂志社办公室室内设计
　　地点：广东 广州
　　时间：2014 年
　　规模：246.86 平方米
　　状态：建成
　　业主：广东生活美学文化传播有限公司

53 深圳壹基金公益基金会总部室内设计
　　地点：广东 深圳
　　时间：2014—2015 年
　　规模：692 平方米
　　状态：建成
　　业主：深圳壹基金公益基金会

54 保利·克洛维时光里商场室内设计
　　地点：广东 广州
　　时间：2014—2015 年
　　规模：3236 平方米
　　状态：建成
　　业主：广州保利商用管理有限公司

55 香港理工大学明日酒店客房国际竞赛
　　地点：香港 九龙
　　时间：2014 年
　　规模：36 平方米
　　状态：方案设计
　　主办方：香港 ICON 酒店

56 紫泥山房
　　地点：广东 广州
　　时间：2015 年
　　规模：133.8 平方米
　　状态：方案设计
　　业主：Cici Chen

54

55

56

62

64

67

57 广州文化馆四小园室内设计
（广府园、广秀园、百果园、翰墨园）
地点：广东 广州
时间：2015—2022 年
规模：9333 平方米
状态：建成
业主：广州市重点公共建设项目管理办公室

58 ISA CHAN 花店室内设计
地点：广东 广州
时间：2015 年
规模：89 平方米
状态：建成
业主：广州伊陈文化活动策划有限公司

59 西场 18 方
地点：广东 广州
时间：2015 年
规模：18 平方米
状态：建成
合作设计：蓝田计划

60 茂名市保利海湾城售楼部室内设计
地点：广东 茂名
时间：2015 年
规模：1223 平方米
状态：建成
业主：茂名和信房地产开发有限公司

61 保利诺丁山售楼部室内设计
地点：广东 佛山
时间：2015—2016 年
规模：780 平方米
状态：建成
业主：佛山市保利昊峰房地产有限公司

62 汕尾金町湾度假别墅
地点：广东 汕尾
时间：2015—2017 年
规模：233 平方米一套，86 平方米七套
状态：建成
业主：汕尾市保利房地产开发有限公司

63 坝光银叶树湿地园科普馆（访客中心）策展方案
地点：广东 深圳
时间：2015 年
规模：1500 平方米
状态：完成
业主：深圳市野生动物救护中心

64 上海半岛酒店高级订制中心室内设计
地点：上海 黄浦
时间：2015—2016 年
规模：240 平方米
状态：建成
业主：佛山市南海川行鞋业有限公司

65 海珠湖国家湿地公园科普体系专业设计
地点：广东 广州
时间：2015 年
状态：建成
业主：海珠湿地管理办公室

66 深圳福田红树林公园布展规划
地点：广东 深圳
时间：2015 年
状态：方案设计
业主：深圳市红树林湿地保护基金会

67 北京大学新太阳学生中心小剧场改造
地点：北京 海淀
时间：2015—2016 年
规模：680 平方米
状态：建成
业主：北京大学

68 广东省话剧院小剧场改造
地点：广东 广州
时间：2015—2017 年
规模：505 平方米
状态：建成
业主：广东省话剧院有限公司

69 广州市越秀区农林街竹丝岗"精品社区"改造设计
地点：广东 广州
时间：2015—2017 年
规模：2220 平方米
状态：方案设计
业主：越秀区农林街道办事处

70 树下——北京大学协作式学习中心
地点：北京 海淀
时间：2016 年
规模：423 平方米
状态：建成
业主：北京大学

69

70

71

72

73

75

76

71 北京大学数学科学学院
　　地点：北京 海淀
　　时间：2016 年至今
　　规模：11174 平方米
　　状态：在建
　　业主：北京大学

72 紫泥十二门无界社区
　　地点：广东 广州
　　时间：2016—2018 年
　　规模：5231 平方米
　　状态：建成
　　业主：广州汇彬物业管理有限公司

73 广州家意投资集团有限公司总部室内设计
　　地点：广东 广州
　　时间：2016 年
　　规模：658 平方米
　　状态：建成
　　业主：广州家意投资集团有限公司

74 吉安庐陵东方宾馆室内设计
　　地点：江西 吉安
　　时间：2016 年
　　规模：1764 平方米
　　状态：建成
　　业主：吉安市庐陵文化旅游开发建设发展有限公司

75 休·比特城寨
　　地点：广东 广州
　　时间：2016 年
　　规模：35000 平方米
　　状态：方案设计
　　业主：广东金展投资管理有限公司

76 北京保利总部大厦大堂艺术品——静谧山水
　　地点：北京 丰台
　　时间：2016 年
　　规模：5000 毫米 ×2000 毫米 ×1120 毫米
　　状态：建成
　　业主：保利（北京）房地产开发有限公司

77 《城市·生长》艺术装置
　　地点：北京 海淀
　　时间：2016—2017 年
　　尺寸：外弧长 12000 毫米，最高约 2800 毫米
　　状态：建成
　　业主：保利（北京）房地产开发有限公司

78 国茶荟"子衿"茶人服饰专营店室内设计
　　地点：广东 广州
　　时间：2016—2017 年
　　规模：747 平方米
　　状态：建成
　　业主：广州国茶荟文化策划有限公司

79 《放飞》艺术装置
　　地点：北京 门头沟
　　时间：2016—2017 年
　　规模：D2000 毫米 ×H7500 毫米、D1500 毫米 ×H4380 毫米、D1000 毫米 ×H3400 毫米
　　状态：建成
　　业主：北京屹泰房地产开发有限公司

80 北京通州保利大都汇写字楼室内设计
　　地点：北京 通州
　　时间：2017—2020 年
　　规模：13757.98 平方米
　　状态：建成
　　业主：保利（北京）房地产开发有限公司

81 一创社艺术季
　　地点：广东 广州
　　时间：2017 年
　　状态：完成
　　业主：广东邦华集团有限公司

82 蓝天里
　　地点：广东 广州
　　时间：2017—2018 年
　　规模：5600 平方米
　　状态：建成
　　业主：广东邦华集团有限公司

83 花都七溪地酒店
　　地点：广东 广州
　　时间：2017 年
　　规模：2400 平方米
　　状态：在建
　　业主：广州市七溪地旅游开发有限公司

84 逸越企业发展有限公司总部室内设计
　　地点：广东 广州
　　时间：2017—2019 年
　　规模：1587.6 平方米
　　状态：建成
　　业主：广州市昇逸置业有限公司

77

78

79

81

82

83

85 白云机场 T2 航站楼 CITIC 中信 PORT 理想家
地点：广东 广州
时间：2017 年
规模：6359 平方米
状态：建成
业主：中信出版集团股份有限公司

86 《川流不息》艺术装置
地点：北京 昌平
时间：2017 年
规模：W1100 毫米 ×H6400 毫米、W750 毫米 ×H4000 毫米、W460 毫米 ×H2600 毫米
状态：建成
业主：北京未来科技城保昌置业有限公司

87 《萌芽》艺术装置
地点：广东 佛山
时间：2017—2018 年
规模：6400 毫米 ×2600 毫米 ×6700 毫米
状态：建成
业主：保利华南实业有限公司

88 星海音乐厅外立面改造
地点：广东 广州
时间：2018 年
规模：5600 平方米
状态：方案设计
业主：广东省星海音乐厅

89 《金色浪潮》艺术装置
地点：广东 广州
时间：2018 年
状态：建成
业主：广东晴波投资有限公司

90 《守望》艺术装置
地点：北京 朝阳
时间：2018—2019 年
规模：H3800 毫米
状态：建成
业主：北京利通房地产开发有限公司

91 中山大学附属第一医院多媒体视像会议中心
地点：广东 广州
时间：2018—2019 年
规模：3915 平方米
状态：建成
业主：同创集团

92 红山村 1302 厂改造
地点：广东 广州
时间：2018 年至今
规模：8000 平方米
状态：在建
业主：吾乡美地（广州）文化旅游投资有限公司

93 碧桂园惠州潼湖科技小镇产业发展中心
地点：广东 惠州
时间：2018 年
规模：1000 平方米
状态：方案设计
业主：惠州碧科科学城发展有限公司

94 齐河保利悦雅酒店
地点：山东 德州
时间：2018—2022 年
规模：13231 平方米
状态：建成
业主：齐河县合筑实业有限公司

95 中国海洋大学崂山校区教学楼树下空间设计
地点：山东 青岛
时间：2018—2019 年
规模：1100 平方米
状态：建成
业主：中国海洋大学

96 海珠湖公园环保办公阿拉善 NGO
地点：广东 广州
时间：2018 年
规模：1816.4 平方米
状态：方案设计
业主：阿拉善

97 清远市保利天汇四期商墅室内设计
地点：广东 清远
时间：2018—2019 年
规模：230 平方米
状态：方案设计
业主：清远鑫瑞房地产有限公司

98 智悦大厦公共区域室内设计
地点：河北 石家庄
时间：2019 年至今
规模：821 平方米
状态：在建
业主：河北保利联创房地产开发有限公司

85

87

88

89

90

91

92

99 青岛保利源诚领秀山领秀海销售中心室内设计
地点：山东 青岛
时间：2019—2020 年
规模：1385 平方米
状态：建成
业主：青岛源诚西海岸置业有限公司

100 保利海陵岛十里银滩 M 区别墅室内设计
地点：广东 阳江
时间：2019—2020 年
规模：365 平方米
状态：建成
业主：保利（海陵岛）房地产开发有限公司

101 总部基地项目 2 号楼样板间室内设计
地点：北京 丰台
时间：2019 年
规模：556 平方米
状态：建成
业主：北京茂丰置业有限公司

102 海珠湿地一期东入口地块改造概念设计咨询
地点：广东 广州
时间：2019 年
规模：15750 平方米
状态：方案设计
业主：海珠湿地维护中心

103 保利梦想城——珑湾花园别墅室内设计
地点：广东 肇庆
时间：2019—2020 年
规模：592 平方米
状态：建成
业主：肇庆保隆置业有限公司

104 佛山保利三水云东海软装设计
地点：广东 佛山
时间：2019 年
规模：809.53 平方米
状态：建成
业主：佛山市三水海都房地产有限公司

105 哥弟家元社区中心
地点：广东 广州
时间：2019 年至今
规模：24000 平方米
状态：在建
业主：广州常元房地产开发实业有限公司

106 廊坊大观广场室内设计
地点：河北 廊坊
时间：2019 年
规模：14000 平方米
状态：建成
业主：新奥文化产业发展有限公司

93

107 上海知识实验室
地点：上海
时间：2020 年
规模：3560 平方米
状态：方案设计
业主：知识实验室

94

108 上海奉贤第一湾规划策划
地点：上海 奉贤
时间：2019 年
规模：3700000 平方米
状态：方案设计
业主：保利置业集团（上海）投资有限公司

102

109 《云水谣》艺术装置
地点：广东 广州
时间：2019 年
规模：φ7000 毫米 ×H7500 毫米
状态：建成
业主：广东保利房地产开发有限公司

105

110 三分宅
地点：菲律宾
时间：2019 年
规模：591 平方米
状态：方案设计
业主：Sandy Fok

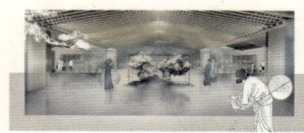
106

111 南沙红港村项目概念策划
地点：广东 广州
时间：2019 年
规模：24553 平方米
状态：方案设计
业主：吾乡美地（广州）文化旅游投资有限公司

107

112 明心康复医疗中心室内设计
地点：广东 广州
时间：2019—2021 年
规模：3389 平方米
状态：建成
业主：广州明心康复医疗中心有限公司

108

113 瓜岭吾乡创艺园
　　地点：广东 广州
　　时间：2019 年至今
　　规模：18647 平方米
　　状态：在建
　　业主：吾乡美地（广州）文化旅游投资有限公司

114 瓜岭古村活化
　　地点：广东 广州
　　时间：2019 年至今
　　规模：7300 平方米
　　状态：在建
　　业主：广州吾乡美地乡村旅游文化发展有限公司

115 清远喜洋洋商业建筑设计
　　地点：广东 清远
　　时间：2019 年
　　规模：23063.19 平方米
　　状态：方案设计
　　业主：清远市弈兴房地产有限公司

116 上海文化广场剧院空间改造设计（一期）
　　地点：上海 黄浦
　　时间：2019 年
　　规模：406 平方米
　　状态：方案设计
　　业主：上海文化广场剧院管理有限公司

117 伍仙桥苏庄大街 29 号
　　地点：广东 广州
　　时间：2019—2020 年
　　规模：1038 平方米
　　状态：建成
　　业主：信走驿

118 中山馨碧花园住宅项目
　　地点：广东 中山
　　时间：2020 年至今
　　规模：398000 平方米
　　状态：在建
　　业主：中山真诚地产开发有限公司

119 天盈广场中达投资办公室室内设计
　　地点：广东 广州
　　时间：2020 年
　　规模：244.5 平方米
　　状态：建成
　　业主：广州市中达投资控股有限公司

120 《垃圾万花筒》艺术装置
　　地点：上海 黄浦
　　时间：2020 年
　　规模：400 毫米 × 600 毫米 × 1550 毫米
　　状态：建成

121 七修健康生活体验空间室内设计
　　地点：河北 廊坊
　　时间：2021 年
　　规模：7996 平方米
　　状态：方案设计
　　业主：廊坊新奥房地产开发有限公司

122 文立方地下多功能活动空间
　　地点：广东 广州
　　时间：2021 年
　　规模：357 平方米
　　状态：建成
　　业主：广东晴波投资有限公司

123 丝绸之路国际文化交流中心 4/5F 餐饮空间
　　地点：河北 廊坊
　　时间：2020 年
　　规模：7100 平方米
　　状态：在建
　　业主：新奥文化产业发展有限公司

124 上海世博会西区规划概念
　　地点：上海 奉贤
　　时间：2021 年
　　规模：838000 平方米
　　状态：方案设计
　　业主：上海盛力置业有限公司

125 保利墨尔本桥街办公建筑室内设计
　　地点：澳洲 墨尔本
　　时间：2021 年
　　规模：961 平方米
　　状态：方案设计
　　业主：保利发展澳大利亚公司

126 荣升街区综合体
　　地点：广东 广州
　　时间：2021 年至今
　　规模：61784 平方米
　　状态：在建
　　业主：广州荣升实业有限公司

113

114

115

116

118

120

124

125

127 四海寒舍——陋室
地点：广东 广州
时间：2021 年至今
规模：420 平方米
状态：在建
业主：四海一家国际美食集团

128 龙洞 111 项目建筑方案设计
地点：广东 广州
时间：2021 年
规模：70440 平方米
状态：方案设计
业主：广州市丽都经贸有限公司

129 樟洞研学基地
地点：广东 清远
时间：2021 年
规模：781.59 平方米
状态：方案设计
业主：华南师范大学附属中学校友会

130 中新知识城新时代文明实践中心精品宫 / 图书馆
地点：广东 广州
时间：2021 年
规模：6000 平方米
状态：建成
业主：广州市黄埔区政府

131 上海市奉贤区文化博物馆建筑景观及室内设计
地点：上海 奉贤
时间：2022 年
规模：6000 平方米
状态：方案设计
业主：上海盛力置业有限公司

132 山泉居餐厅改造
地点：广东 佛山
时间：2022 年
规模：564 平方米
状态：在建
业主：佛山市南海区西樵山泉居茶艺有限公司

133 黄沙水产交易市场策划及建筑概念设计
地点：广东 广州
时间：2022 年
规模：16130 平方米
状态：方案设计
业主：广州粤恒丰水产品综合批发市场有限公司

134 慈云喜舍书院概念设计
地点：广东 广州
时间：2022 年
规模：363 平方米
状态：方案设计
业主：慈云喜舍

135 会元中学
地点：广东 广州
时间：2021—2022 年
规模：58757 平方米
状态：方案设计
业主：广州市黄埔区政府

136 海心沙二号花城苑
地点：广东 广州
时间：2022 年至今
规模：1930 平方米
状态：在建
业主：花城苑

137 学有空间
地点：广东 广州
时间：2022 年至今
规模：827 平方米
状态：方案设计
业主：广州学有文化发展有限公司

138 顺德容桂住宅
地点：广东 顺德
时间：2022 年
规模：557 平方米
状态：方案设计
业主：王先生

139 连南三排古寨民宿改造设计项目
地点：广东 清远
时间：2022 年
规模：3500 平方米
状态：方案设计
业主：眺阅旅游管理（清远）有限责任公司

126

128

129

130

133

135

136

后记
Postscript

2016年冬，我在"一席"的演讲第一次以"无界"诠释扉：指打开两个空间边界的连通器。2017年，我和艺术家宋冬合作，开始"无界博物馆"计划，菜市场美术馆正是这个计划的其中一个项目。

何谓"无界"？正因为我们每天都处于"有界"的世界里——我们的学习有学科之界，我们的工作有部门之界，后疫情时代更无处不是界。现代科学正是对事物进行分门别类才迅速发展起来让更多人认识、了解世界。但最终如果不跨越这些界别定义，认知便无法更新，学科便无法发展。于是，"跨界"成了创新的代名词，而我们提的"无界"更接近于回归事物的本原。

世上本没有博物馆，当把那些被专家认定为有价值的物品集中在一个地方并加以解读便出现了博物馆。菜市场为何不能是博物馆？豆子可以做出多少种副食品？以"鱼"字为偏旁的字你又认识多少个？在有限的空间里，菜应该怎么摆才能吸引更多的人？近年来，通过"菜市场美术馆""民众花园""移动美术馆"等一系列拓展美术馆、博物馆边界和定义的空间实践，我们让很多先前从来不敢踏入美术馆的普通人真正意识到"人人都是艺术家"不是空话。例如，菜市场的摊主们从独善其身到自我觉醒，成为连接社区的黏合剂和社区营造的主导者。

所有以上这些艺术营造和社区实践一直在持续推动"无界社区"的形成，这也是扉建筑最为重要的设计理念。人类本就是群居动物，问题是为何要群居？因为只有互帮互助、相互守望才能更好地一起生活。但今天我们住的小区房，我们常常不知道邻居的状况，更谈不上邻里关系。所以，"无界社区"探讨的是一个可以适应不同尺度下的一个熟人社会的样本，一个能够相互连接的居住群落。

当然，同那些提供大量公共空间（例如共享厨房、共享洗衣房、共享客厅……）的共享住宅不同，"无界社区"没有这种严格意义上的"公共"空间。每个住户都有一个可自建的"边缘空间"，在拥有私密性的基础上鼓励人们和左邻右舍开展其乐融融的邻里生活和公共活动。这种无界，不是说完全没有界，而是更接近人类群居生活的本原——相互守望、彼此联结，从而最终在空间、心理、文化、生活方式，以及价值观的认知上包容和尊重各自的边界。

"无界"是一种境界，没有分别心，没有你我，这是万事万物之源。特别感谢宋冬老师在扉美术馆实现了他个人最大尺寸的作品"无界之墙"，从而开启我们一系列走向无界的创作。

感谢所有在扉建筑、扉美术馆工作的同事。

2022年10月

In the winter of 2016, in my speech on Yixi platform, I used the concept of "borderless" to explain FEI (literally meaning "portal" in Chinese) for the first time: a connecting vessel that opens the border between two spaces. In 2017, I started the Borderless Museum Program in cooperation with artist Song Dong, and the Market Museum is part of the program.

Why is "borderless" raised? It is precisely because we live in a "bordered" world every day—there are different disciplines in academia, various departments in workplace and in the post-epidemic era, borders are even more prevalent. In fact, modern science develops rapidly by classifying things so that more people can cognize and understand the world. But in the end, if we do not cross the borders between definitions, we can never keep our cognition up to date and develop the disciplines. As a result, "cross-border" has become a synonym for innovation, and the "borderless" concept is closer to returning to the origin of things.

In the beginning, there was no museum in the world; museums appeared when the objects considered valuable were collected in a certain place to be interpreted by experts. Why can't the wet market be a museum? How many kinds of non-staple food can be made beans? How many Chinese characters do you know that contain the radical "fish"? In a limited space, how should the vegetables be arranged to attract more buyers? In recent years, through a series of spatial practices such as Market Museum, People's Garden and Moving Arts Museum which expand the boundaries and definitions of art galleries and museums, we have made many ordinary people who never dared to enter art galleries realize that "everyone is an artist" is not empty talk. For example, the stall owners of the wet market have awakened and stepped out of their own little world to bridge the differences in the community and become the dominant force behind community empowerment.

It is the above-mentioned artistic creation and community practices that have been continuously promoting the formation of "borderless community", which is also the most important design concept of FEI Architects. Humans are social animals. The question is why we should live together. Because only by helping and watching out for each other can we live together for the better. Today we live in a community, but often do not know the situation of our neighbors, let alone neighborhood relations. Therefore, what "borderless community" explores is a sample of acquaintance society that can adapt to different scales, and a residential community that allows everyone to connect with each other.

Of course, unlike shared housing, which provides a lot of common space (such as shared kitchen, laundry and living room, etc), "borderless community" does not have such "public" space in a strict sense. However, each household has a self-built "marginal space" to encourage and develop happy neighborhood life and public activities on the basis of reserving their own privacy. This kind of "borderless" doesn't mean that there is no border at all, but is closer to the origin of human social life, where people watch out for and connect with each other, so as to ultimately accommodate and respect every individual's boundary in space, psychology, culture, lifestyle as well as values and norms.

"Borderless" is an ideal state of mind, which surpasses all differences and bridges the gap between people. It is the origin of everything. We are especially grateful to Mr. Song Dong for installing his largest work "Borderless Wall" in FEI Arts Museum, which kicked off a series of works towards the ultimate "borderless".

I would like to express my sincere gratitude to all the colleagues who have worked in FEI Architects and FEI Arts.

October, 2022

致谢

特别感谢何镜堂、许安之两位恩师在百忙之中拨冗为本书亲笔作序。

紫泥十二门无界社区：

投资管理方：广州汇彬物业管理有限公司

施工负责人：汪志超及团队

设计团队：米笑、岳靓、刁家俊、曹锦添、卓锦万、雷清月、许思琪、黄宇城、毕晓璇、程结成、杨国安、李颖诗、文洁霞、伊凡 Ivan Blasco、宋定侃

竹丝岗无界社区：

农林菜市场 44 位摊主

"手美术馆"艺术家华南理工大学建筑学院马增锋

广州竹丝岗社区街坊

"菜市场美术馆"mapping 工作坊所有学生

扉美术馆团队及工作小组主要成员(按姓氏拼音排列)：杜惠、黄锐、黄晓彤、江俊颖、康洁、雷君瑜、李佳岭、李自若、梁靖、廖宝欣、莫庆珊、彭雪莹、邱燕霞、谭涵丹、曾希翎、张晓琳、郑嘉如、朱旭飞

顾问：群岛 Archipelago

编辑：周芹

资料整理：岳靓、代巧玲、肖晓芸

封面设计：臧立平 @typo_d

版式设计：江俊颖、曾莹、何志森

插图：曾莹、代巧玲

图片处理：吴玉婵

摄影：郑庆龄、丘、Tony Metaxas、孙婷婷、廖禧臻、彭雪莹、黄毅、许愿、许思琪、龙伟豪、肖晓芸、何志森

翻译：程倩、曾希翎、何志森

校对：米笑、何志森、王童渝、李嘉惠、莫庆珊、廖胜昌

Acknowledgement

Special thanks to my kind teachers, He Jingtang and Xu Anzhi, who took their precious time out of busy schedules to write the prefaces for this book.

Borderless Community of Zi Ni Twelve Portals:

Property Owner: Guangzhou Huibin Property Management Co., LTD

Construction Manager: Wang Zhichao and his team

Design Team: Michelle Yip, Yue Liang, Diao Jiajun, Cao Jintian, Zhuo Jinwan, Lei Qingyue, Xu Siqi, Huang Yucheng, Bi Xiaoxuan, Cheng Jiecheng, Yang Guoan, Li Yingshi, Wen Jiexia, Ivan Blasco, Song Dingkan

Borderless Community of Zhusigang:

44 stall owners of the Nonglin Market

Artist of "Hands Museum", Ma Zengfeng from School of Architecture, South China University of Technology

Residents of the Guangzhou Zhusigang Community

All the Mapping Workshop students participating in the Market Museum Project

Key members of the FEI Arts team and working group (in alphabetic order of Chinese surname): Du Hui, Huang Rui, Huang Xiaotong, Jiang Junying, Kang Jie, Lei Junyu, Li Jialing, Li Ziruo, Liang Jing, Liao Baoxin, Mo Qingshan, Peng Xueying, Qiu Yanxia, Tan Handan, Zeng Xiling, Zhang Xiaolin, Zheng Jiaru, Zhu Xufei

Consultant: Archipelago

Editor: Zhou Qin

Information Collation: Yue Liang, Dai Qiaoling, Xiao Xiaoyun

Cover Design: Zang Liping@typo_d

Layout Design: Jiang Junying, Zeng Ying, Jason Zhisen Ho

Illustration: Zeng Ying, Dai Qiaoling

Image Processing: Wu Yuchan

Photography: Zheng Qingling, Qiu, Tony Metaxas, Sun Tingting, Liao Xizhen, Peng Xueying, Huang Yi, Xu Yuan, Xu Siqi, Long Weihao, Xiao Xiaoyun, Jason Zhisen Ho

Translation: Eline Cheng, Zeng Xiling, Jason Zhisen Ho

Proofreading: Michelle Yip, Jason Zhisen Ho, Wang Tongyu, Li Jiahui, Mo Qingshan, SC Liu

关于扉

扉，指门户、边界。源自《道德经》(第十一章)："凿户牖以为室，当其无，有室之用。故有之以为利，无之以为用。"

扉深耕于中国南方，以扉建筑为空间实践的载体，以扉美术馆为研究平台，通过"艺术营造"的设计理念致力于城市社区性的建构，把每一栋建筑都变成一座无界社区。

扉建筑

通过探讨建筑空间的边界，建造符合地区自然与人文环境的建筑。设计的扉美术馆、紫泥十二门无界社区、二沙文立方、星海音乐厅系列改造、例外·方所等均成为广州文艺地标。以 FEI (F—Functionality, 功用为本; E—Elegance, 简的艺术; I—Infinity, 无限可能) 为理念，在地为用之本，大道至简，突破专业边界持续学习的态度让我们在模糊空间边界到模糊专业边界的过程中持续创新。

扉美术馆

一家致力于通过艺术营造来探讨社会性和公共性，不断丰富美术馆空间、公共艺术之定义的民营美术馆。

扉于 2007 年在广州东山口竹丝岗社区创立了扉艺廊，2017 年更名为扉美术馆。现今已成为华南地区开馆历史最长、极具影响力的民营非牟利当代艺术机构。近年来，扉美术馆通过各种公众参与艺术项目探索当代艺术的在地性、公共性和社会性，让艺术深入日常。

工作方法：艺术营造

以建筑艺术无界为核心理念，通过加强人与环境、人与场所、人与人的关联，使城市永续发展。

对扉建筑而言，艺术营造是在完美解决使用功能和空间美学的同时，还能够关注建筑周边生活环境和居民生活方式的改善，关注社会关系的重构和社区的活化，关注城市空间的社会性和公共性的改善，关注大众对艺术审美和创新精神的认知拓展。在此意义上每一个设计都具有公共艺术性，每一个设计过程都可以变成一次由各方利益介入参与互动的策展过程，每一个建筑都可以是艺术营造。

对扉美术馆而言，艺术营造是推动当代艺术发展的一个策展方向，也是一种有别于传统"白盒子"美术馆封闭内向的展览方式。艺术营造理念强调的不是艺术作品本身，而是艺术作品和周边环境、场所、使用者及各方利益的关系，思考了艺术作品如何向普通日常生活学习和回归，以及如何通过深入日常生活的艺术作品建立艺术与生活的连接。

建筑与艺术的融合也让扉看到建筑设计不只是一个局限在红线内的建造，而是使用者和日常生活息息相关的一个在地艺术的营造过程。这就是扉对建筑和当代艺术的理念。

About FEI

"FEI" in Chinese refers to the door or the border. *Tao Te Ching* Chapter 11 writes: "When doors and windows are cut out, from the interior vacancy arises the utility of a room. Therefore, what has a positive existence serves for profitable adaptation, and what has not that for actual usefulness."

FEI is deeply rooted in the south of China. Taking FEI Architects as vehicle for space practice and FEI Arts Museum as research platform, and devoting itself to the construction of urban community guided by "Artecture" design concept, it endeavors to turn every building into a borderless community.

FEI Architects

By exploring the boundary of architectural space, we intend to construct buildings that fit in both the natural and cultural environments. FEI Arts, the Borderless Community of Zi Ni Twelve Portals, Ersha Island MAN LAP FONG, Xinghai Concert Hall series, and Exception·Fangsuo Commune have all become literary and artistic landmarks of Guangzhou. Guided by the principles of FEI ((F—Functionality, which is the basis; E—Elegance, i.e., the art of simplicity; I—Infinity, i.e., infinite possibilities), emphasizing down-to-earth as the basis for functionality and the simplest way as the best way, and with the attitude of breaking through the professional boundary to continue learning, we constantly make innovations in the process from blurring spatial boundary to blurring professional boundary.

FEI Arts

FEI Arts is a private art gallery devoted to exploring sociality and publicness through art intervention, and constantly extending the definitions of art gallery space and public art.

In 2007, FEI Gallery was founded by FEI in the Zhusigang Community of Dongshankou, Guangzhou, and was renamed as FEI Arts in 2017. Now it has been among the oldest and most influential private non-profit contemporary art institutes in South China. In recent years, the Museum has explored the locality, publicity and sociality of contemporary art through various art projects featuring public participation with a view to bring art into the daily life of ordinary people.

Approach to Work: Artecture

With Artecture as the core concept and by strengthening the connections between people and environment, people and places as well as people and people, we strive to achieve sustainable development of the city.

For FEI Architects, Artecture not only perfectly achieves functional utility and space aesthetics, but is also concerned with the improvement of living environment and residents' lifestyle around the building, the reconstruction of social relations and the activation of the community, the improvement of the sociality and publicness of urban space as well as the public's cognitive expansion of aesthetics and innovative spirit. In this sense, every design has its public artistry, every design process can become an interactive curatorial process involving all the stakeholders, and every building can be artecture.

For FEI Arts, Artecture is both a curatorial direction to promote contemporary art and an exhibition approach destinguished from the traditional inward-looking "white box". Artecture emphasizes not the artwork itself, but the dynamic relationship between the artwork and the surrounding environment, venues, users and all stakeholders. It considers how should artworks learn and return to ordinary daily life as well as how to establish the connection between art and life through artworks deeply rooted in everyday life.

The integration of architecture and art makes us realize that architectural design is not just construction confined within the red line, but a process of constructing site-specific art reflecting the close relation between the users and their daily life. This is our understanding of architecture and contemporary art.

与扉一起，打造无界未来

Let's create a borderless future together with FEI